Langenscheidt

Universal-Phrasebook French

Edited by the
Langenscheidt Editorial Staff

Langenscheidt

Berlin · Munich · Vienna · Zurich
London · Madrid · New York · Warsaw

Phonetic Transcriptions: The Glanze Intersound System
Illustrations: Kirill Chudinskiy

Neither the presence nor the absence of a designation that any entered word constitutes a trademark should be regarded as affecting the legal status of any trademark.

ISBN 978-3-468-98985-8
© 2011 Langenscheidt KG, Berlin and Munich
Printed in Germany

11010

1   HUMAN RELATIONS

4 FOOD AND DRINK

5 SIGHTSEEING

8 POST OFFICE, BANK, INTERNET

9 EMERGENCIES

HOW TO FIND IT

This phrasebook contains all of the most important expressions and words you'll need for your trip. They have been divided up according to situation and organised into 10 chapters. The page borders have been colored to help you find things even more quickly.

Each chapter consists of example sentences and lists of words together with complementary vocabulary. This will help you put together exactly the right sentence you need for any situation. The easy-to-understand basic grammar section will give you further support.

Of course you can just show the person you're talking to the French translation of the sentence you wish to say. But the easily distinguished blue phonetic alphabet will enable you to speak your chosen phrase without any knowledge of French whatsoever. In order to give you an indication of the proper intonation, we have inserted punctuation marks into the phonetic spellings.

For vital situations we have also included sentences that go from French to English, so that a French person may also be able to communicate with you.

In order to cover as many different situations as possible we offer alternatives with many sentences; these are written in italics and separated by a slash:

Shall we get together *tomorrow/this evening*?

Si on se voyait *demain/ce soir*?

sē ôN sə vô·âye *dəmeN/sə sô·ä*?

You can separate the alternatives into individual sentences, asking either

| Shall we get together tomorrow? | **Si on se voyait demain?** |
| | sē ôN sə vô·äye dəmeN? |

or

| Shall we get together this evening? | **Si on se voyait ce soir?** |
| | sē ôN sə vô·äye sə sô·är? |

When we offer more than two possibilities there will be an ellipsis at that point in the sentence; the possible phrases to complete your sentence will be listed underneath:

| I'd like a seat ... | **J'aimerais avoir une place ...** |
| | zhāməre ävô·är ēn pläs ... |

by the window.	**fenêtre.** fənet'rə.
in nonsmoking.	**non-fumeurs.** nôN-fēmär.
in smoking.	**fumeurs.** fēmär.

You can then put them together as needed, for example:

| I'd like a seat in smoking. | **J'aimerais avoir une place fumeurs.** |
| | zhāmərə ävô·är ēn pläs fēmär. |

Often you will also find sentence completions in parentheses. You can include these in your communication as you like.

| Can you take me (a part of the way) there? | **Vous pouvez m'emmener (un bout de chemin)?** vōō pōōvā mämnā (eN bōōdshəmeN)? |

If you wish to have someone take you the full way there, simply leave out **un bout de chemin**.

There are two equivalents in French of the English *you* (and *your*), depending on whether you are talking to a close friend or a child (in which case you say **tu**) or to someone you do not know or are merely acquainted with (where you use **vous**). We generally give the more formal **vous** form in the example sentences. Sometimes, however, particularly in the section on Human Relations, the differentiation can be very important. In such cases both forms are given, e.g.:

What's your name?	**Comment *vous appelez-vous/tu t'appelles?*** kômäN *vōōzáplā-vōō/tẹ täpeĺ?*

In French the form of the word used is sometimes dependent upon the gender of either the person speaking or the person addressed. In cases in which these forms make a difference in the pronunciation, we have indicated the different forms by the symbols ♂ (masculine) and ♀ (feminine):

I already have plans.	**Je suis déjà ♂ pris/♀ prise.** zhə svē dāzhä ♂ prē/♀ prēz.

A man would say **Je suis déjà pris**; a woman would say **Je suis déjà prise**.

In French, nouns and their qualifying adjectives belong to either the masculine or feminine gender, and the articles differ accordingly. In cases where you can't identify the correct gender from the article (**l'** and **les**), we have used the abbreviations *m* for masculine and *f* for feminine words in the word lists. We have included the feminine endings with the adjectives only when they are irregular. You will find the rules for the regular endings in the basic grammar section of this book.

11

HOW DO YOU PRONOUNCE IT?

All words and phrases are accompanied by simplified pronunciation. The sound symbols you find in **Langenscheidt's Universal Phrasebooks** are the symbols you are familiar with from your high-school or college dictionaries of the *English* language.

For French, these basic symbols are supplemented mainly by ā, ē and N. These three sounds have no English equivalents and have to be learned by listening.

Vowels

Symbol	Approximate Sound	Examples
ä	The *a* of *father*.	**madame** mädäm **garage** gäräzh **tasse** täs
ā	The *a* of *fate* (but without the "upglide").	**été** ātā
ā̲	A sound that has to be learned by listening: round the lips for the *o* of *nose*; then, without moving the lips, try to pronounce the *a* of *fate*.	**deux** dā̲ **œuf** ā̲f **fleur** flā̲r
e	The *e* of *met*.	**adresse** ädres
ē	The *e* of *he*.	**midi** mēdē **dire** dēr

Symbol	Approximate Sound	Examples
ē	A sound that has to be learned by listening. Round the lips for the *o* of *nose*; then, without moving the lips, try to pronounce the *e* of *he*.	**fumer** fēmā **le fumeur** lə fēmār
ō	The *o* of *nose*, but without the "upglide".	**rideau** rēdō **rôle** rōl
ô	The *o* of *often*. In French, sometimes shorter, as in *moment*; sometimes longer, as in *sport*.	**moment** mômäN **sport** spôr
ōō	The *u* of *rule*, but without the "upglide".	**trou** trōō **rouge** rōōzh
ə	The neutral sound (unstressed): the *a* of *ago* or the *u* of *focus*.	**je** zhə **demi** dəmē
N	This symbol does not stand for a sound but shows that the preceding vowel is nasal – is pronounced through nose and mouth at the same time. Nasal sounds have to be learned by listening.	**temps** täN **nom** nôN **matin** mäteN **parfum** pärfeN

Symbol	Approximate Sound	Examples
	Try not to use the *ng* of *sing* in their place.	

Consonants

Symbol	Approximate Sound	Examples
g	The *g* of *go*.	**gare** gär
l	The *l* of *love* (not of fall).	**voler** vôlā
ng	The *ng* of *sing*. (Occurs in some foreign words in French.)	**parking** pärkēng
r	The French "fricative" *r*. It is similar to the *j* of Spanish *Juan* and softer than the *ch* of Scottish *loch* or German *Bach*.	**rue** rē̄ **rire** rēr
s	The *s* of *sun* (not of *praise*).	**salle** säl **garçon** gärsôN
sh	The *sh* of *shine*.	**chapeau** shäpō
v	The *v* of *vat*.	**avant** ävāN
y	The *y* of *year*.	**payer** pāyā **avion** ävyôN
z	The *z* of *zeal* or the *s* of *praise*.	**blouse** blōōz

14

Symbol	Approximate Sound	Examples
zh	The *s* of *measure* or the *si* of *vision*.	**jour** zhŏŏr **genou** zhənŏō

The symbols b, d, f, k, m, n, p, and t are basically pronounced as in *boy, do, far, key, me, no, pin,* and *toy,* respectively.

The syllables of a French word are usually stressed evenly, with slightly more emphasis on the last syllable of a word or sentence. Therefore, stress is not indicated in this sound system – except in the following four situations in which the last syllable is not only stress-free but is barely pronounced as a syllable.

This absence of stress is shown through a preceding accent mark:

'ē: ē'ē   as in **fille** fē'ē

e'ē   as in **bouteille** bōōte'ē or **appareil** äpäre'ē

ä'ē   as in **paille** pä'ē

ā'ē   as in **feuille** fā'ē

ōō'ē   as in **grenouille** grənōō'ē.

'lə: b'lə   as in **table** täb'lə

k'lə   as in **siècle** syek'lə

g'lə   as in **triangle** trē·äNg'lə.

'rə   as in **libre** lēb'rə or **quatre** kät'rə or **descendre** däsäNd'rə

n'yə   as in **ligne** lēn'yə or **campagne** käNpän'yə.

Combinations like the following are pronounced as a single "gliding" sound:

ô·ä   as in **roi** rô·ä or **voyage** vô·äyäzh

15

ô·eN   as in **loin** lô·eN

yeN   as in **bien** byeN

ē̲·ē   as in **nuit** nē̲·ē or **conduire** kôNdē̲·ēr

o͞o·ē   as in **oui** o͞o·ē or **weekend** o͞o·ēkend

o͞o·e   as in **souhaiter** so͞o·etā

The final sound of a word is often linked with the initial sound of the next: **il y a** ēlyä, and a silent consonant may then become pronounced: **ils** ēl **+ on** ôN = ēlzôN. This transition, called "liaison," is used quite frequently in French, but only the most important and common cases are rendered in this phrasebook. (As you progress in French, you will learn to use "liaison" with great frequency.)

A raised dot separates two neighboring vowel symbols: **réalité** rā·älētā. This dot is merely a convenience to the eye; it does not indicate a break in pronunciation.

Try to produce French sounds by speaking at the front of the mouth, with vigorous movement of the lips, unlike English, which is spoken in the back of the mouth, and with "lazy" lips.

Human Relations

HI AND BYE

Good morning.	**Bonjour!** bôNzhōōr!
Good afternoon.	**Bonjour!** bôNzhōōr!
Good evening.	**Bonjour!, Bonsoir!** bôNzhōōr!, bôNsô·är!
Good night.	**Bonsoir!** bôNsô·är!
Hello.	**Salut!** sälē!

INFO In France people say **bonjour** for "good morning" and "hello," as well as in the evening to greet someone, as with "good evening." One may also use **bonsoir** to greet someone very late in the evening; otherwise it is used to say goodbye to someone in the evening. **Bonsoir** is also used to say "good night"; **bonne nuit** is only used with children.

Do you mind if I sit here?	**Est-ce que je peux m'asseoir ici avec *vous/toi*?** eskə zhə pā mäsô·är ēsē ävek vōō/tô·ä?
I'm sorry, but I'm afraid this seat is taken.	**Non, malheureusement, c'est occupé.** nôN, mälārāsmäN, setôkēpā.
How are you?	***Comment allez-vous/Comment vas-tu?*** kômäNtälāvōō/kômäN vä-fē?
I'm sorry, but I have to go now.	**Je suis désolé, mais je dois partir maintenant.** zhə svē dāzôlā, me zhə dô·ä pärtēr meNtnäN.

Good-bye.	**Au revoir!** ō rəvô·är!
See you *soon/ tomorrow.*	**A *bientôt/demain*!** ä byeNtō/dəmeN!
Bye!	**Salut!** sälē!
Nice to have met you.	**Je suis ♂ heureux/♀ heureuse d'avoir fait *votre/ta* connaissance.** zhə svē ♂ ārā/♀ ārāz dävô·är fe vôt'rə/ta kônesäNs.
Thank you, I had a lovely evening.	**Merci pour cette charmante soirée.** mersē pōōr set shärmäNt sô·ärā.
Have a good trip.	**Bon voyage!** bôN vô·äyäzh!

SMALL TALK ...

... about yourself and others

| What's your name? | **Comment *vous appelez-vous/tu t'appelles*?** kômäN vōōzäplā-vōō/tē täpel? |

INFO In speaking to each other, the French use two different forms of "you" to distinguish between individual intimate friends and children – **tu** – and groups of people, lesser-known acquaintances, and strangers – **vous**. Use **vous** – the polite and plural form – for speaking with an adult outside of your family unless he/she indicates otherwise. Offering the use of first names is not an invitation to use the familiar form **tu**. Men are addressed simply as **Monsieur**, women as **Madame** or **Mademoiselle**, without the last name.

My name is ...	**Je m'appelle ...** zhə mäpel ...
Where are you from?	**D'où *venez-vous/viens-tu*?** dōō vənā-vōō/vyeN-tē?
I'm from ...	**Je viens de...** zhə vyeN də ...
Are you married?	**Est-ce que *vous êtes/tu es* marié?** eskə vōōzet/tē e märyā?
Do you have any children?	**Est-ce que *vous avez/tu as* des enfants?** eskə vōōzävā/tē ä däzäNfäN?
Do you have any brothers or sisters?	**Est-ce que *vous avez/tu as* des frères et sœurs?** eskə vōōzävā/tē ä dā frer ā sär?
I have a *sister/brother*.	**J'ai *une sœur/un frère*.** zhā ēn sär/eN frer.
How old are you?	**Quel âge *avez-vous/as-tu*?** keläzh ävä-vōō/ä-tē?
I'm ... years old.	**J'ai ... ans.** zhā ... äN.
What is your line of work?	**Qu'est-ce que *vous faites/tu fais* comme travail?** keskə vōō fet/tē fe kôm trävä'ē?
I'm a(n) ...	**Je suis ...** zhə svē ...

Is this your first time here?	**C'est la première fois que *vous venez/tu viens*?** se lä prəmyer fô-ä kə vōō vənä/tē vyeN?
No, I was in France ... time(s) before.	**Non, c'est la ... fois que je viens en France.** nôN, se lä ... fô-ä kə zhə vyeN äNfräNs.
How long have you been here?	***Vous êtes/Tu es* là depuis combien de temps déjà?** vōōzät/tē e lä dəpē-ē kôNbyeN də täN dāzhä?
For ... *days/weeks* now.	**Depuis ... *jours/semaines*.** dəpē-ē ... zhōōr/səmen.
How much longer will you be staying?	***Vous restez/Tu restes* encore combien de temps ici?** vōō restā/tē rest äNkôr kôNbyeN də täN ēsē?
I'm leaving tomorrow.	**Je pars demain.** zhə pär dəmeN.
Another *week/two weeks*.	**Encore *une semaine/quinze jours*.** äNkôr ēn semen/keNz zhōōr.
How do you like it here?	**Ça *vous/te* plaît ici?** sä vōō/tə ple ēsē?
I like it very much.	**Ça me plaît beaucoup.** sä mə ple bōkōō.
Have you seen ... yet?	**Est-ce que *vous avez/tu as* déjà vu ...?** eskə vōōzävä/tē ä dāzhä vē ...?

Have you ever been to America?	***Vous êtes/Tu es*** **déjà allé aux États-Unis?** vōōzet/t͡ē e dāzhā älā ōzātäzē͡nē?
You should visit me if you come to America some day	**Si vous allez un jour aux États-Unis, venez donc me voir.** sē vōōzälā eN zhōōr ōzätäzē͡nē, vənā dôN mə vô·är.
You're welcome to stay at my house.	**Tu peux coucher chez moi. Cela me ferait plaisir.** t͡ē pä kōōshā shā mô·ä. səlä mə fərə plezēr.
I'd be happy to show you the city.	**Je me ferai un plaisir de** ***vous/te*** **montrer la ville.** zhə mə fərā eN plāzēr də *vōō/te* môNtrā lä vēl.

SOCIALIZING

Would you like to ...?

What are you doing tomorrow?	**Qu'est-ce que** ***vous faites/tu fais*** **demain?** keskə *vōō fet/t͡ē fe* dəmeN?
Shall we get together *tomorrow/this evening*?	**Si on se voyait** ***demain/ce soir*?** sē ôN sə vô·äye *dəmeN/sə sô·är*?
Yes, I'd like that.	**Avec plaisir.** ävek plāsēr.
I'm sorry, but I already have plans.	**Ce n'est malheureusement pas possible. Je suis déjà ♂ pris/♀ prise.** sə ne mäl͡ārāzmäN pä pôsēb'lə. zhə svē dāzhā ♂ prē/♀ prēz.

Would you like to join me for dinner this evening?	**Si on dînait ensemble ce soir?** sē ôN dēnā äNsäNb'lə sə sô·är?

■ *Dining with Friends (p. 109), Going out in the Evening (p. 191)*

I'd like to invite you to ...	**Je voudrais *vous inviter/t'inviter* à ...** zhə vōōdre vōōzeNvētā/teNvētā ä ...
When/Where shall we meet?	**On se donne rendez-vous *à quelle heure/où*?** ôN sə dôn räNdāvōō ä kelār/ōō?
Let's meet at ... o'clock.	**Disons qu'on se rencontre à ... heures.** dēzôN kôN sə räNkôNträ ... ār.
I'll pick you up at ... o'clock.	**Je passerai *vous/te* prendre à ... heures.** zhə päsrā vōō/te präNdrä ... ār.
Shall I see you again?	**On va se revoir?** ôN vä sə rəvô·är?

No, thanks

I already have plans.	**J'ai déjà quelque chose de prévu.** zhā dāzhä kelkə shōz də prāvū.
I'm waiting for someone.	**J'attends quelqu'un.** zhätäN kelkeN.
Leave me alone!	**Laissez-moi tranquille!** lesā-mô·ä träNkēl!
Get lost!	**Casse-toi!** käs-tô·ä!

23

COMMUNICATING

Does anyone here speak English?	**Il y a ici quelqu'un qui parle anglais?** ēlyä ēsē kelkeN kē pärl äNgle?
? **Vous parlez français?** vōō pärlā fräNse?	Do you speak French?
Only a little.	**Un petit peu seulement.** eN pətē pā sālmäN.
Please speak a little slower.	**Parlez plus lentement, s'il vous plaît.** pärlā plē läNtmäN, sēl vōō ple.
? **Vous comprenez?/Tu comprends?** vōō kôNprənä/tē kôNpräN?	Do you understand?
I understand.	**J'ai compris.** zhā kôNprē.
I didn't understand.	**Je n'ai pas compris.** zhə nā pä kôNprē.
Would you please repeat that?	**Vous pourriez répéter, s'il vous plaît?** vōō pōōryā rāpātā, sēl vōō ple?
What is this called in French?	**Comment ça s'appelle en français?** kômäN sä säpel äN fräNse?
What does ... mean?	**Que signifie ...?** kə sēnyēfē ...?

24

WHAT DO YOU THINK?

It *was/is* very nice here.	**C'était/C'est très agréable ici.** sāte/se trezägrä·äb'lə ēsē.
Great!	**Très bien!** tre byeN!
Wonderful!	**Magnifique!** mänyēfēk!
Fantastic!	**Formidable!** fôrmēdäb'lə!
I like that.	**Ça me plaît.** sä mə ple.
With great pleasure.	**Très volontiers.** tre vôlôNtyā.
OK.	**O.K.** ōkā.
It's all the same to me.	**Ça m'est égal.** sä metāgäl.
Whatever you like.	**Comme vous voulez.** kôm vōō vōōlā.
I don't know yet.	**Je ne sais pas encore.** zhə nə se päzäNkôr.
Maybe.	**Peut-être.** pātet'rə.
Probably.	**Probablement.** prôbäbləmäN.
Too bad!	**Dommage!** dômäzh!
I'm afraid that's impossible.	**Ce n'est malheureusement pas possible.** sə ne mälārāzmäN pä pôsēb'lə.
I'd rather ...	**J'aimerais mieux ...** zheməre myä ...
I don't like that.	**Ça ne me plaît pas.** sä nə mə ple pä.

25

No.	**Non.** nôN.
Absolutely not.	**En aucun cas.** äNōkeN kä.
No way!	**Pas question!** pä kestyôN!

BASIC PHRASES

Please; Thank you

Could you please help me?	**Est-ce que vous pourriez m'aider?** eskə vōō pōōryā mādā?

INFO In French, to reply "Yes, please" to an offer such as "Would you like another cup of coffee?," one would say **"Oui, merci."** or **"Oui, volontiers."** To answer a request such as "May I use your telephone?," say **"Oui, je vous en prie."**

Yes, please.	**Oui, volontiers.** ōō-ē, vôlôNtyā.
No, thank you.	**Non, merci.** nôN, mersē.
Thank you very much.	**Merci beaucoup.** mersē bōkōō.
That was very nice of you.	**C'était très aimable de votre part.** sāte trezemäb'lə də vôt'rə pär.
You're welcome.	**Je vous en prie.** zhə vōōzäN prē.
My pleasure.	**Il n'y a pas de quoi.** ēlnyä pä də kvä.
May I?	**Vous permettez?** vōō permetā?

I'm sorry.

Excuse me!	***Excusez-moi/Excuse-moi!*** ekskē̄zā-mô-ä/ekskē̄s-mô-ä!
Sorry about that.	**Je suis désolé.** zhə svē dāzôlā.
It was a misunder-standing.	**C'était un malentendu.** sāteteN mäläNtäNdē̄.

Best wishes

Congratulations!	**Meilleurs vœux!** meyār vā!
Happy birthday!	**Joyeux anniversaire!** zhô-äyā̄ änēverser!
Get well soon!	**Bon rétablissement!** bôN rātäblēsmäN!
Good luck!	**Bonne chance!** bôn shäNs!
Have a good trip!	**Bon voyage!** bôN vô-äyäzh!
Have fun!	**Amusez-vous bien!** ämē̄zā-vōō byeN!
Merry Christmas!	**Joyeux Noël!** zhô-äyā̄ nô-el!
Happy New Year!	**Une bonne et heureuse année!** ē̄n bôn ā ā̄rāz änā!

FOR THE HANDICAPPED

I'm physically handicapped.

Je suis handicapé physique.
zhə svē äNdēkäpä fēsēk.

Could you please help me?

Vous pourriez m'aider, s'il vous plaît?
vōō pōōryä mädä, sēl vōō ple?

Do you have a wheelchair for me?

Est-ce que vous avez un fauteuil roulant pour moi? eskə vōōzävä eN fōtụ̈'ē rōōläN pōōr mô·ä?

Where is the nearest elevator?

Où est l'ascenseur le plus proche?
ōō e läsäNsụ̈r lə plệ prôsh?

Could you please take my luggage to the room?

Est-ce que vous pouvez transporter mes bagages dans ma chambre?
eskə vōō pōōvä träNspôrtä mā bägäzh däN mä shäNb'rə?

Is it suitable for wheelchairs?

Est-ce que c'est aménagé pour recevoir les handicapés en fauteuil roulant? eskə setämänäzhä pōōr resevô·är läzäNdēkäpä äN fōtụ̈'ē rōōläN?

Is there a ramp there for wheelchairs?

Est-ce qu'il y a une rampe pour les fauteuils roulants? eskēlyä ēn räNp pōōr lä fōtụ̈'ē rōōläN?

Where is a restroom for handicapped?

Où sont les toilettes pour handicapés?
ōō sôN lā tô·älet pōōr äNdēkäpä?

I need someone to come with me.

J'ai besoin de quelqu'un qui m'accompagne. zhā bəzô·eN də kelkeN kē mäkôNpän'yə.

Human relations

address	**l'adresse** *f* lädres
alone	**seul** sāl
to arrive	**arriver** ärēvā
boyfriend	**l'ami** *m* lämē
brother	**le frère** lə frer
child	**l'enfant** *m* läNfäN
city	**la ville** lä vēl
daughter	**la fille** lä fē'ē
father	**le père** lə per
friend *(male)*	**l'ami** *m* lämē
friend *(female)*	**l'amie** *f* lämē
girlfriend	**l'amie** *f* lämē
to go dancing	**aller danser** älā däNsā
to go out to eat	**aller manger** älā mäNzhā
academic high school	**le lycée** lə lēsā
husband	**le mari** lə märē
to invite	**inviter** eNvētā
job	**la profession** lä prôfesyôN
to leave	**partir** pärtēr
to like *(I would like to)*	**aimer** āmā
to like *(it appeals to me)*	**plaire** pler
to make a date	**se donner rendez-vous** sə dônā räNdāvōō
married	**marié** märyā

to meet *(get to know)*	**faire la connaissance de** fer lä kônesäNs də
to meet up with someone	**se rencontrer** sə räNkôNtrā
mother	**la mère** lä mer
no	**non** nôN
old	**âgé** äzhā
photograph	**la photo** lä fōtō
to repeat	**répéter** rāpātā
to return	**revenir** rəvnēr
school	**l'école** *f* lākôl
to see again	**revoir** rəvô·är
brothers and sisters	**les frères et sœurs** *m/pl* lā frer ā sār
sister	**la sœur** lä sār
son	**le fils** lə fēs
to speak	**parler** pärlā
student *(male)*	**l'étudiant** *m* lātēdyäN
student *(female)*	**l'étudiante** *f* lātēdyäNt
to study	**faire des études** fer dāzātēd
to take *(someone)* home	**raccompagner** räkôNpänyā
to understand	**comprendre** kôNpräNd'rə
vacation	**les vacances** *f/pl* lä väkäNs
to wait	**attendre** ätäNd'rə
wife	**la femme** lä fäm
to write down	**noter** nôtā
yes	**oui** ōō·ē

BUSINESS CONTACTS

On the Phone

➡️ *see also: Communicating (p. 24)*

This is ... from ...	**Allô! Ici ♂ Monsieur/♀ Madame ...,**	
	de la maison ... älô! ēsē ♂ məsyā/	
	♀ mädäm ... də lä mesôN ...	

| I would like to speak to ... | **Je voudrais parler à ...** zhə vōōdre pärlā ä ... | |

| ❗ | **Ne quittez pas.** nə kētā pä. | I'll connect you. |

| ❗ | **... est en ligne en ce moment.** ... etäN lēn'yə äN sə môMäN. | ... is busy at the moment. |

| ❗ | **... n'est pas là aujourd'hui.** ... ne pä lä ōzhōōrdvē. | ... is not here today. |

| ❓ | **Désirez-vous laisser un message?** dāzērā-vōō lāsā eN mäsäzh? | Would you like to leave a message? |

At the Reception Desk

| I'm here to see Mr./Ms. ... | **Je voudrais voir *Monsieur/Madame ...*** zhə vōōdre vô·är məsyā/mädäm ... |

| My name is ... | **Je m'appelle ...** zhə mäpel ... |

| I have an appointment with ... at ... o'clock. | **J'ai un rendez-vous avec ...., à ... heures.** zhā eN räNdāvōō ävek ..., ä ... ār. |

| ! | **Un instant, s'il vous plaît.** | One moment, please. |
| | eNeNstäN, sēl vōō ple. | |

| ! | **... arrive tout de suite.** | ... will be right here. |
| | ... ärēv tōōtsvēt. | |

| ! | **... est encore en conférence.** | ... is still in a meeting. |
| | ... etäNkôr äN kôNfäräNs. | |

| ! | **Si vous voulez bien venir avec moi.** sē vōō vōōlā byeN venēr ävek mô-ä. | Would you come with me, please? |

| ? | **Veuillez patienter un instant, s'il vous plaît.** väyā päsyäNtā eNeNstäN, sēl vōō ple. | Would you please wait here a moment? |

| ? | **Est-ce que je peux vous apporter un café?** eske zhe pä vōōzápôrtā eN käfā? | Would you like a coffee? |

At Trade Fairs

I'm looking for the ... booth.	**Je cherche le stand de l'entreprise ...** zhe shersh le stäNd de läNtreprēz ...
Do you have any information about ...?	**Vous avez de la documentation sur ...?** vōōzävä de lä dôkēmäNtäsyôN sēr ...?
Do you also have pamphlets in English?	**Vous avez aussi des prospectus en anglais?** vōōzävä ôsē dā prôspektēs äNäNgle?

1

address	**l'adresse** *f* lädres
appointment	**le rendez-vous** lə räNdā-vōō
booth	**le stand** lə stäNd
brochures	**la documentation** lä dôkēmäNtäsyôN
building	**le bâtiment** lə bätēmäN
to call on the tele-	**téléphoner** tālāfônā
phone	
catalog	**le catalogue** lə kätälôg
convention	**le congrès** lə kôNgre
corporation	**le groupe industriel** lə grōōp eNdēstrē·el
conference	**la conférence** lä kôNfäräNs
– room	**la salle de conférence** lä säl də kôNfäräNs
copy	**la photocopie** lä fōtōkôpē
client	**le client** lə klē·äN
department	**le service** lə servēs
– head	**le chef de service** lə shef də servēs
documents	**les documents** *m/pl* lā dôkēmäN
earphones	**le casque** lə käsk
fax machine	**le téléfax** lə tālāfäks
hall *(auditorium)*	**le hall** lə äl
information	**l'information** *f* leNfôrmäsyôN
interpreter	**l'interprète** *m, f* leNterpret
management	**la direction** lä dēreksyôN
manager	**le gérant** lə zhäräN
to meet	**rencontrer** räNkôNträ
meeting *(discussion)*	**la conférence** lä kôNfäräNs

meeting *(get-together)*	**la rencontre** lä räNkôNt'rə
news	**le message** lə mäsäzh
office	**le bureau** lə bēŗō
photocopier	**le photocopieur** lə fōtōkôpyär
price	**le prix** lə prē
– list	**la liste des prix** lä lēst dā prē
prospectus	**le prospectus** lə prôspektēs
reception	**la réception** lä räsepsyôN
representative	**le représentant** lə rəpräzäNtäN
secretary	**la secrétaire** lä səkräter
session	**la séance** lä sā·äNs
speech	**l'exposé** *m* lekspōzā
telephone	**le téléphone** lə tālāfôn

Accommodations

INFORMATION

Where is the tourist information office?	**Où se trouve l'office du tourisme?** ōō sə trōōv lôfēs dē tōōrēsm?

INFO The tourist information office (**office du tourisme**) will be happy to supply you with information about hotels, guest houses and rooms to rent in family homes.

Could you recommend a ...	**Vous pourriez me recommander ...** vōō pōōryā rəkômäNdä ...
good hotel?	**un bon hôtel?** eN bônôtel?
inexpensive hotel?	**un hôtel pas trop cher?** eNôtel pä trō sher?
boarding house?	**une pension?** ēn päNsyôN?
room at a private home?	**une location chez l'habitant?** ēn lôkäsyôN shā läbētäN?
I'm looking for accommodation ...	**Je cherche une chambre ...** zhə shersh ēn shäNb'rə ...
in a central location.	**centrale.** säNträl.
in a quiet location.	**dans un cadre tranquille.** däNzeN käd'rə träNkēl.
at the beach.	**sur la plage.** sēr lä pläzh.
How much will it cost (approximately)?	**Quel est le prix (à peu près)?** kel ā lə prē (ä pē pre)?
Can you make a reservation for me there?	**Vous pourriez réserver pour moi?** vōō pōōryā rāzervā pōōr mô·ä?

Is there a *youth hostel/* *camping ground* here?	**Est-ce qu'il y a** *une auberge de jeunesse/un terrain de camping* **par ici?** eskēlyä ēn ôbärzh də zhānes/eN tereN də känpēng pär ēsē?
Is it far from here?	**C'est loin d'ici?** se lô·eN dēsē?
How do I get there?	**Comment est-ce que je peux m'y rendre?** kômäN eskə zhə pē̄ mē räNd'rə?
Could you draw me a map?	**Vous pourriez me dessiner le chemin?** vōō pōōryā mə dāsēnā lə shəmeN?

2

HOTEL AND VACATION RENTAL

Hotel

Do you have a *double/* *single* room available ...	**Vous auriez une chambre pour** *deux personnes/une personne* **...** vōōzôryā ēn shäNb'rə pōōr dā̲ persôn/ēn persôn ...
for *one night/* *... nights?*	**pour** *une nuit/... nuits?* pōōr ēn nē̲-ē̲/... nē̲-ē̲?
with a *full bathroom/shower* and toilet?	**avec** *bain/douche* **et WC?** ävek beN/dōōsh ā dōōbləvā-sā?
with a balcony?	**avec balcon?** ävek bälkôN?

Malheureusement, nous	I'm sorry, but we're
sommes complets. mälärãzəməN,	booked out.
nōō sôm kôNple.	

I have a reservation.	**On a retenu chez vous une chambre à**
My name is ...	**mon nom. Je m'appelle ...** ônä rətənē
	shä vōō ēn shäNb'rə ä môN nôN. zhə
	mäpel ...

| Here is my confirma- | **Voici ma confirmation.** |
| tion. | vô·äsē mä kôNfērmäsyôN. |

INFO Most double rooms in France have double beds. If
you need separate beds, you must ask for **lits
jumeaux** when reserving a double room.

The **cabinet de toilette** is a small chamber with a sink and sometimes a shower or toilet that is separated from the rest of the room
by a wall. If the price of the room includes a **cabinet de toilette**,
you should ask whether that includes a shower. The prices are
always given by room.

| How much will it | **Combien ça coûte ...** |
| cost ... | kôNbyeN sä kōōt ... |

with/without	***avec/sans** le petit déjeuner?*
breakfast?	ävek/säN lə pətē dāzhānā?
with *half/full*	**avec la *demi-pension/pension com-***
board?	***plète?*** ävek lä dəmēpäNsyôN/
	päNsyôN kôNplet?

| May I have a look at | **Je pourrais voir la chambre?** |
| the room? | zhə pōōre vô·är lä shäNb'rə? |

Do you have a ... room?	**Vous auriez encore une chambre ...** vōōzôryā äNkôr ẽn shäNb'rǝ ...
less expensive	**meilleur marché?** meyär märshā?
larger	**plus grande?** plē gräNd?
quieter	**plus tranquille?** plē träNkēl?
It's very nice. I'll take it.	**Elle me plaît. Je la prends.** el mǝ ple. zhǝ lä präN.

? **Avez-vous des bagages?**
ävävōō dā bägäzh?

Do you have any luggage?

Can you have my luggage brought to the room?	**Vous pourriez apporter mes bagages dans la chambre?** vōō pōōryā äpôrtā mā bägäzh däN lä shäNb'rǝ?
Can you have a crib put in the room?	**Vous pourriez installer un lit d'enfant?** vōō pōōryā eNstälā eN lē däNfäN?
Where can I park my car?	**Où est-ce que je peux garer ma voiture?** ōō eskǝ zhǝ pā gärā mä vô·ätēr?
Where are the showers?	**Où sont les douches?** ōō sôN lā dōōsh?
When are the meals served?	**Quelles sont les heures des repas?** kel sôN lāzär dā rǝpä?
Where can we get breakfast?	**Où peut-on prendre le petit déjeuner?** ōō pātôN präNd'rǝ lǝ pǝtē dāzhānā?

2

Can I give you my valuables for safe-keeping?	**Est-ce que je peux vous confier mes objets de valeur?** eskə zhə pä vōō kôNfyä mäzôbzhe də välär?
I'd like to pick up my valuables.	**Je voudrais reprendre mes objets de valeur.** zhə vōōdrä rəpräNd'rə mäzôbzhe də välär.
Can you exchange money for me?	**Est-ce que vous pouvez me changer de l'argent?** eskə vōō pōōvä mə shäNzhä dəlärzhäN?
May I have the key to room ..., please?	**La clé de la chambre ..., s'il vous plaît.** lä klä dəlä shäNb'rə ..., sēl vōō ple.
Can I make a call to America (from my room)?	**Est-ce que je peux téléphoner aux États-Unis (depuis ma chambre)?** eskə zhə pä täläfônä ōzätäzēnē (dəpē·ē mä shäNb'rə)?
Is there any mail/Are there any messages for me?	**Est-ce qu'il y a *du courrier/un message* pour moi?** eskēlyä dē kōōryä/eN mäsäzh pōōr mô·ä?
I'd like a wakeup call (tomorrow) at ... o'clock, please.	**Réveillez-moi (demain) à ... heures, s'il vous plaît.** rävāyā-mô·ä (dəmeN) ä ... ār, sēl vōō ple.
We're leaving tomorrow.	**Nous partons demain.** nōō pärtôN dəmeN.
Would you please prepare my bill?	**Préparez-nous la note, s'il vous plaît.** präpärā-nōō lä nôt, sēl vōō ple.

We really liked it here.	**Nous avons passé un séjour très agréable.** nōōzävôN päsā eN sāzhōōr trezägrā·äb'lə.

May I leave my luggage here until ... o'clock?	**Est-ce que je peux encore laisser mes bagages ici jusqu'à ... heures?** eskə zhə pä äNkôr lāsā mā bägazh ēsē zhēskä ... ār?

Would you call a taxi for me, please?	**Appelez-moi un taxi, s'il vous plaît.** äplā-mô·ä eN täksē, sēl vōō ple.

Vacation Rental

We have rented the apartment ...	**Nous avons loué l'appartement ...** nōōzävôN lōō·ā läpärtəmäN ...

Where can we pick up the keys?	**Où pouvons-nous prendre les clés?** ōō pōōvôN-nōō präNd'rə lā klā?

Could you please explain how the ... works?	**Vous pourriez nous expliquer comment fonctionne ..., s'il vous plaît?** vōō pōōryā nōōzeksplēkā kômäN fôNksyôn ... sēl vōō ple?

stove	**la cuisinière** lä kē̄·ēsēnyer
dishwasher	**le lave-vaisselle** lə läv-vesel
washing machine	**la machine à laver** lä mäshēn ä lävā

Where is the fuse box?	**Où se trouvent les fusibles?** ōō sə trōōv lā fēsēb'lə?

Where is the meter?	**Où se trouve le compteur électrique?**
	oō sə troōv lə kôNtạr ālektrēk?
Where do we put the trash?	**Où devons-nous déposer les ordures?**
	oō dəvoN-noō dāpōzā lāzôrdēr?
Where can I make a phone call?	**Où est-ce qu'on peut téléphoner ici?**
	oō eskoN pạ tālāfōnā ēsē?
Could you tell us where we might find ...	**Pouvez-vous nous dire où il y a ...**
	poōvā-voō noō dēr oō ēlyä ...

a bakery?	**une boulangerie?** ēn boōläNzhərē?
the nearest bus stop?	**le prochain arrêt de bus?**
	lə prôshenāre də bẽs?
a grocery store?	**une alimentation?**
	ēn älēmäNtäsyôN?

Complaints

➡ *Please; Thank you (p. 26)*

The *shower/light* doesn't work.	**La douche/lumière ne marche pas.**
	lä dōōsh/lẽmyer nə märsh pä.
The toilet doesn't flush.	**La chasse d'eau ne marche pas.**
	lä shäs dō nə märsh pä.
There is no (hot) water.	**Il n'y a pas d'eau (chaude).**
	ēlnyä pä dō (shōd).

42

Could I please have ...?	**Est-ce que je pourrais avoir encore ..., s'il vous plaît?** eskə zhə pōōre ävô-är äNkôr ..., sēl vōō ple?

another blanket	**une couverture** ēn kōōvertēr
some more dish towels	**des torchons** dā tôrshôN
another towel	**une serviette** ēn servyet
a few more clothes hangers	**quelques cintres** kelkə seNt'rə

2

I can't lock the door to my room.	**Ma porte ne ferme pas à clé.** mä pôrt nə ferm päzäklā.
The window doesn't *open/close*.	**La fenêtre ne *s'ouvre/ferme* pas.** lä fənet'rə nə sōōv'rə/ferm pä.
The faucet drips.	**Le robinet goutte.** lə rôbēne gōōt.
The drain is stopped up.	**L'écolement est bouché.** lākōōlmäN e bōōshā.
The toilet is stopped up.	**Les WC sont bouchés.** lā dōōblevə-sā sôN bōōshā.

Hotel and Vacation Rental

adapter	**l'adaptateur** *m* lädäptätār
additional costs	**les charges** *f/pl* lā shärzh
apartment	**le studio** lə stēdyō
balcony	**le balcon** lə bälkôN
bathroom	**la salle de bains** lä säl də beN
bathtub	**la baignoire** lä benyô-är

bed	**le lit** lə lē
– linens	**les draps** *m/pl* lā drä
-sheet	**le drap** lə drä
-side lamp	**la lampe de chevet** lä läNp də shəve
-spread	**le couvre-lit** lə kōōv'rə-lē
bill	**la facture** lä fäktēr
blanket	**la couverture en laine** lä kōōvertēr äN len
breakfast	**le petit déjeuner** lə pətē dāzhānā
– buffet	**le buffet petit déjeuner** lə bēfe pətē dāzhānā
broken	**cassé** käsā
broom	**le balai** lə bäle
cabin	**le bungalow** lə beNgälō
chair	**la chaise** lä shez
cleaning products	**les produits** *m/pl* **de nettoyage** lā prôdē̄-ē də netô-äyäzh
closet	**le placard** lə pläkär
cold water	**l'eau** *f* **froide** lō frô-äd
complaint	**la réclamation** lä rāklämäsyôN
crib	**le lit d'enfant** lə lē däNfäN
cup	**la tasse** lä täs
departure	**le départ** lə dāpär
deposit	**la caution** lä kôsyôN
dinner	**le dîner** lə dēnā
dirty	**sale** säl
dishes	**la vaisselle** lä vesel
dishwasher	**le lave-vaisselle** lə läv-vesel
door	**la porte** lä pôrt

door lock	**la serrure** lä serēr
double room	**la chambre pour deux personnes**
	lä shäNb're pōōr dœ persŏn
down-payment	**l'acompte** *m* läkôNt
drinking water	**l'eau potable** lō pôtäb'le
electricity	**l'électricité** *f* lälektrēsētä
elevator	**l'ascenseur** *m* läsäNsār
extension cable	**la rallonge électrique**
	lä rälôNzh älektrēk
final cleaning	**le ménage de fin de séjour**
	le mänäzh de feN de säzhōōr
floor	**l'étage** *m* lätäzh
first –	**le rez-de-chaussée** le räd-shōsä
flush	**la chasse d'eau** lä shäs dō
full price	**le prix T.T.C.** le prē tä-tä-sä
full room and board,	**la pension complète**
European plan	lä päNsyôN kôNplet
fuse	**le fusible** le fēzēb'le
gas cylinder	**la bouteille de butane**
	lä bōōte'e̅ de bētän
glass	**le verre** le ver
high season	**la haute saison** lä ōt sezôN
hot water	**l'eau** *f* **chaude** lō shōd
hotel	**l'hôtel** *m* lōtel
key	**la clé** lä klä
lamp	**la lampe** lä läNp
light bulb	**l'ampoule** *f* läNpōōl
lost	**perdu** perdē
low season	**la basse saison** lä bäs sezôN

45

luggage	**les bagages** *m/pl* lā bägäzh
lunch	**le déjeuner** lə dāzhᾱnā
maid	**la femme de chambre** lä fäm də shäNb'rə
mattress	**le matelas** lə mätlä
outlet	**la prise (de courant)** lä prēz (də kōōräN)
pillow	**l'oreiller** *m* lôrāyā
plate	**l'assiette** *f* läsyet
plug	**la fiche** lä fēsh
pool	**la piscine** lä pēsēn
pre-season	**l'avant-saison** *f* läväN-sezôN
reception	**la réception** lä rāsepsyôN
refrigerator	**le réfrigérateur** lə räfrēzhärätᾱr
rent	**le loyer** lə lô-äyā
to rent	**louer** lōō-ā
(rented vacation) apartment	**le meublé** lə mᾱblā
(rented vacation) house	**la maison de vacances** lä mezôN də väkäNs
to reserve	**réserver** rāzervā
reserved	**réservé** rāzervā
room	**la chambre** lä shäNb'rə
– inventory	**l'état** *m* **des lieux** lātä dā lē-ᾱ
– with half board	**la demi-pension** lä dəmē-päNsyôN
shower	**la douche** lä dōōsh
single room	**la chambre pour une personne** lä shäNb'rə pōōr ᾱn persôn
sink *(bathroom)*	**le lavabo** lə läväbō

46

sink *(kitchen)*	**l'évier** *m* lāvyā
stairs	**les escaliers** *m/pl* lāzeskälyā
stopped up	**bouché** bōōshā
table	**la table** lä täb'əl
tax on visitors	**la taxe de séjour** lä täks də sāzhōōr
telephone	**le téléphone** lə tālāfôn
toilet	**les toilettes** *f/pl* lā tô-älet
– paper	**le papier hygiénique** lə päpyā ēzhē-ānēk
towel	**la serviette** lä servyet
trash	**les ordures** *f/pl* lāzôrdēr
– can	**la poubelle** lä pōōbel
to wake	**réveiller** rāvāyā
water	**l'eau** *f* lō
– faucet	**le robinet** lə rôbēne
window	**la fenêtre** lä fənet'rə
to work	**fonctionner** fôNksyônā

YOUTH HOSTEL, CAMPING

Youth Hostel

Is there anything available?	**Est-ce que vous avez encore quelque chose de libre?** eskə vōōzävä äNkôr kelkə shōz də lēb'rə?
I would like to stay for *one night* / ... *nights*.	**Je voudrais rester** *une nuit*/... *nuits*. zhə vōōdre restā ēn nē·ē/... nē·ē.
How much will it cost for one night?	**Combien coûte une nuit?** kôNbyeN kōōt ēn nē·ē?

Do you also have double rooms?	**Vous avez aussi des chambres pour deux personnes?** vōōzävä ôsē dā shäNb'rə pōōr dā persòn?
Is breakfast included?	**Le petit déjeuner est compris?** lə pətē dāzhānā ā kôNprē?
How much does ... cost?	**Combien coûte le ...** kôNbyeN kōōt lə ...
breakfast lunch dinner	**petit déjeuner?** pətē dāzhānā? **déjeuner?** dāzhānā? **dîner?** dēnā?
Where is the dining room?	**Où est la salle à manger?** ōō e lä säl ä mäNzhā?
Where can I buy something *to eat/ to drink*?	**Où est-ce qu'on peut acheter quelque chose à *manger/boire* ici?** ōō eskôN pā äshtā kelkə shōz ä *mäNzhā/bô·är* ēsē?
Where are the meals served?	**Quelles sont les heures des repas?** kel sôN lāzär dā rəpä?
Where are the bathrooms?	**Où sont les lavabos?** ōō sôN lā läväbō?
Where is the restroom?	**Où sont les toilettes?** ōō sôN lā tô·älet?
Where can I do my laundry?	**Où est-ce qu'on peut laver son linge?** ōō eskôN pā lävā sôN leNzh?

When do I have to be back by?	**Jusqu'à quelle heure est-ce qu'on peut rentrer le soir?** zhēskä kelär eskôN pā räNtrā lə sô·är?
Do you have any lockers?	**Il y a des casiers fermant à clé?** ēlyä dā käzyā fermäNtä klā?
What's the best way to get to the middle of town?	**Quel est le meilleur moyen pour aller dans le centre?** kel e lə meyär mô·äyeN pōōr älä däN lə säNt'rə?

Camping

May we camp on your property?	**Est-ce que nous pouvons camper sur votre terrain?** eskə nōō pōōvôN käNpä sēr vôt'rə tereN?
What is the charge for ...	**Quel est le tarif pour ...** kel e lə tärēf pōōr ...
a car with a trailer?	**une voiture avec caravane?** ēn vô·ätēr ävek kärävän?
a camping van?	**un camping-car?** eN käNpēng-kär?
a tent?	**une tente?** ēn täNt?
We'd like a (sheltered) place in the shade.	**Nous voudrions un emplacement à l'ombre (abrité du vent).** nōō vōōdrē·ôN eNäNpläsmäN älôNb'rə (äbrētā dē väN).
We'd like to stay *one night/... nights.*	**Nous voudrions rester *un jour/... jours.*** nōō vōōdrē·ôN restā eN zhōōr/... zhōōr.

2

49

Where are the bathrooms?	**Où sont les lavabos?** ōō sôN lā lävåbō?
Where is the rest room?	**Où sont les toilettes?** ōō sôN lā tô-älet?
Where can I ...	**Où est-ce qu'on peut ...** ōō eskôN pā ...
empty the chemical waste from the toilet?	**vidanger les WC chimiques?** vēdäNzhā lā dōōblevä-sā shēmēk?
empty sewage water?	**se débarrasser des eaux usées?** sə dābäräsä dāzō ēzā?
fill the tank with fresh water?	**refaire le plein d'eau?** rəfer lə pleN dō?
Can I use electricity?	**Vous avez un branchement électrique?** vōōzävā eN bräNshmäN ālektrēk?
Is there a grocery store here?	**Est-ce qu'il y a une alimentation par ici?** eskēlyä ēn älēmäNtäsyôN pär ēsē?
Can I *rent/exchange* gas cylinder here?	**Je peux *emprunter/échanger* des bouteilles de butane ici?** zhə pā äNpreNtā/āshäNzhā dā bōōte'ē də bētän ēsē?
May I borrow a(n) ..., please?	**Vous pourriez me prêter ..., s'il vous plaît?** vōō pōōryā mə prātā ..., sēl vōō ple?

air mattress	**le matelas pneumatique** lə mätlä pnā̲mätēk
bed linens	**les draps** *m/pl* lā drä
to borrow	**emprunter** äNpreNtā
camping	**le camping** lə käNpēng
– permit	**la carte de camping** lä kärt də käNpēng
campsite	**le terrain de camping** lə tereN də käNpēng
check-in	**la déclaration de séjour** lä dāklärä̲syôN də sāzhōōr
to cook	**faire la cuisine** fer lä kē̲-ēzēn
cooking utensils	**les ustensiles** *m/pl* **de cuisine** läzē̲stáNsēl də kē̲-ēzēn
detergent	**la lessive** lä lesēv
dormitory	**le dortoir** lə dôrtô-är
electrical outlet	**la prise (de courant)** lä prēz (də kōōräN)
electricity	**le courant (électrique)** lə kōōräN (ālektrēk)
foam (insulation)	**le matelas mini-mousse** lə mätlä mēnē-mōōs
mat	
gas	**le gaz** lə gäz
– canister	**la cartouche de gaz** lä kärtōōsh də gäz
– cylinder	**la bouteille de butane** lä bōōtā'ē də bḙtän
group of kids	**le groupe de jeunes** lə grōōp də zhän
hostel father	**le père aubergiste** lə per ōberzhēst

2

51

hostel mother	**la mère aubergiste** lä mer ōberzhēst
to iron	**repasser** rəpäsā
mallet	**le maillet** lə mäye
playground	**le terrain de jeux** lə tereN də zhā
rental fee	**les frais** *m/pl* **d'utilisation** lā fre dᵉtēlēzäsyôN
reservation	**la réservation** lä rāzervāsyôN
room	**la chambre** lä shäNb'rə
shower	**la douche** lä dōōsh
site	**l'emplacement** *m* läNpläsmäN
sleeping bag	**le sac de couchage** lə säk də kōōshäzh
stove	**le réchaud** lə rāshō
tent	**la tente** lä täNt
– peg	**le piquet (de tente)** lə pēke (də täNt)
– pole	**le mât de tente** lə mä də täNt
toilet	**les toilettes** *f/pl* lä tô·älet
to wash	**laver** lävā
washing machine	**la machine à laver** lä mäshēn ä lävā
washroom	**les lavabos** *m/pl* lā läväbō
water	**l'eau** *f* lō
– canister	**le jerricane à eau** lə dzherēkän ä ō
youth hostel	**l'auberge** *f* **de jeunesse** lōberzh də zhānes
– card	**la carte d'auberge de jeunesse** lä kärt dōberzh də zhānes

On the Way

ASKING THE WAY

Excuse me, where is ...?	**Pardon, où est ...?** pärdôN, ōō e ...?	
How can I get to ...?	**Pour aller à ...?** pōōr älā ä ...?	
What's the *quickest/cheapest* way to get to the ...	**Quel est le moyen** *le plus rapide/le moins cher* **pour aller ...** kele lə mô·äyeN *lə plē räpēd/lə mô·eN sher* pōōr älä ...	
train station?	**à la gare?** ä lä gär?	
bus station?	**à la gare routière?** ä lä gär rōōtyer?	
airport?	**à l'aéroport?** ä lä·ārōpôr?	

! **Le mieux, c'est de prendre un taxi.** lə myā, se də präNd(rə) eN täksē.

The best thing to do is take a taxi.

! **Là-bas.** lä-bä.

Over there.

! **En arrière.** äNäryer.

Go back.

! **Tout droit.** tōō drô·ä.

Straight ahead.

! **A droite.** ä drô·ät.

To the right.

! **A gauche.** ä gōsh.

To the left.

54

!	**La _première/deuxième_ rue à _gauche/droite_.** lä prəmyer/ däzyem rē ä gōsh/drô·ät.	The _first/second_ street to the _left/right_.
!	**Au feu.** ō fȩ̄.	At the traffic lights.
!	**Après le carrefour.** äpre lə kärfōōr.	After the intersection.
	Traversez ... träversā ...	Cross ...
!	**le pont.** lə pôN.	the bridge.
	la place. lä pläs.	the square.
	la rue. lä rē.	the street.
!	**Après, vous redemanderez.** äpre, vōō rədəmäNdrā.	When you get there, ask again.
	Vous pouvez prendre ... vōō pōōvā präNd'rə ...	You can take ...
!	**le bus.** lə bēs.	the bus.
	le tramway. lə trämōō·ā.	the streetcar.
	le RER. lə er-ə-er.	the commuter train.
	le métro. lə mātrō.	the subway.

Is this the road to ...?	**C'est bien la route de ...?** se byeN lä rōōt də ...?	
How far is it?	**C'est à quelle distance?** setäkel dēstäNs?	
!	**Assez loin.** äsā lô·eN.	Pretty far.

55

! **Pas loin.** pä lô·eN.   Not (very) far.

How many minutes will it take to walk?	**Combien de minutes à pied?** kôNbyeN də minēt ä pyā?
Could you show it to me on the map?	**Vous pouvez me le montrer sur la carte, s'il vous plaît?** vōō pōōvā me lə môNtrā sēr lä kärt, sēl vōō ple?

Asking the Way

bridge	**le pont** lə pôN
to cross	**traverser** träversā
curve	**le virage** lə vēräzh
intersection	**le carrefour** lə kärfōōr
road	**la route** lä rōōt
straight ahead	**tout droit** tōō drô·ä
street	**la rue** lä rē
to the left	**à gauche** ä gōsh
to the right	**à droite** ä drô·ät
traffic lights	**le feu** lə fā

AT THE BORDER

Passport Control

! **Vos papiers, s'il vous plaît.** vō päpyā, sēl vōō ple.   May I see your documents, please?

! **Votre passeport, s'il vous plaît.** vôt'rə päspôr, sēl vōō ple.   May I see your passport, please?

! **Votre passeport est périmé.**
vôt'rə päspôr e pārēmä.

Your passport is
expired.

I'm with the ... group. **Je fais partie du groupe ...**
zhə fe pärtē dü grōōp ...

Customs

? **Avez-vous quelque chose à
déclarer?** ävā-vōō kelkə shōz ä
däklärä?

Do you have anything
to declare?

! **Ouvrez votre *coffre*/*valise*, s'il
vous plaît.** ōōvrā vôt'rə *kôf'rə*/
vä lēz, sēl vōō ple.

Open your *trunk*/*suit-
case*, please.

! **Vous devez le déclarer.**
vōō dəvā lə däklärā.

You have to declare
that.

3

At the Border

bill	**la facture** lä fäktēr
border	**la frontière** lä frôNtyer
car registration	**les papiers** *m/pl* **de voiture** lä päpyä də vô·ätēr
country identifica- tion sticker	**la plaque de nationalité** lä pläk də näsyônälētä
customs	**la douane** lä dōō·än
– declaration	**la déclaration de douane** lä däklärä·syôN də dōō·än
– office	**le bureau de douane** lə bērō də dōō·än
date	**la date** lä dät

57

to declare	**déclarer** dāklārā
driver's license	**le permis de conduire**
	lə permē də kôNdē̲·ēr
first name	**le prénom** lə prānôN
ID	**la carte d'identité** lä kärt dēdäNtētā
inoculation record	**le carnet de vaccination**
	lə kärne də väksēnäsyôN
invalid	**pas valable** pä väläb'lə
last name	**le nom de famille** lə nôN də fämē'ē
nationality	**la nationalité** lä näsyônälētā
number	**le numéro** lə nēmārō
papers	**les papiers** *m/pl* lā päpyā
passport	**le passeport** lə päspôr
– control	**le contrôle des passeports**
	lə kôNtrôl dā päspôrt
place of residence	**le domicile** lə dômēsēl
to renew	**prolonger** prôlôNzhā
signature	**la signature** lä sēnyätēr
tour group	**le groupe (de touristes)**
	lə grōop (də tōorēst)
valid	**valable** väläb'lə
value-added tax (VAT)	**la TVA** lä tā-vā-ä

LUGGAGE

May I *leave/pick up* my luggage here?
Je voudrais *laisser mes bagages ici/retirer mes bagages*. zhə vōōdre lāsā mā bägäzh ēsē/rətērā mā bägäzh.

May I leave my backpack with you *for an hour/until ...?*
Est-ce que je peux laisser mon sac à dos ici *pour une heure/jusqu'à ...?* eskə zhə pä lāsā môN säk ä dō ēsē pōōr ēnār/zhēskä ...?

I'd like to have these bags sent to ...
Je voudrais faire enregistrer ces bagages pour ... zhə vōōdre fer äNrzhēstrā sā bägäzh pōōr ...

When will they be at ... ?
Quand seront-ils à ...? käN sərôNtēl ä ...?

My luggage hasn't arrived (yet).
Mes bagages ne sont pas (encore) arrivés. mā bägäzh nə sôN pä (äNkôr) ärēvā.

Where is my luggage?
Où sont mes bagages? ōō sôN mā bägäzh?

A suitcase is missing.
Il manque une valise. ēl mäNk ēn välēz.

My luggage has been damaged.
Ma valise a été abîmée. mä välēz ä ātā äbēmā.

Who can I report it to?
A qui est-ce que je peux m'adresser? äkē eskə zhə pä mädräsā?

59

backpack	**le sac à dos** lə säk ä dō
bag	**le sac** lə säk
baggage claim	**le retrait des bagages** lə rətre dā bägäzh
baggage ticket	**le bulletin d'enregistrement** lə bēlteN däNrzhēstrəmäN
carry-on luggage	**les bagages** *m/pl* **à main** lā bägäzh ä meN
excess luggage	**l'excédent** *m* **de bagages** leksädäN də bägäzh
flight bag	**le sac de voyage** lə säk də vô·äyäzh
to hand in	**faire enregistrer** fer äNrzhēstrā
locker	**la consigne automatique** lä kôNsēnyôtômätēk
luggage	**les bagages** *m/pl* lā bägäzh
– check-in	**l'enregistrement** *m* **des bagages** läNrzhēstrəmäN dā bägäzh
– storage	**la consigne** lä kôNsēn'yə
to pick up	**retirer** rətērā
suitcase	**la valise** lä välēz

PLANE

Information and Booking

Where is the ... counter?	**Où est le guichet de ...?** ōō e lə gēshe də ...?
When is the next flight to ...?	**A quelle heure est le prochain vol pour ...?** äkelār e lə prôsheN vôl pōōr ...?

When will a plane be flying to ... *today/ tomorrow*?	**A quelle heure y a-t-il *aujourd'hui/ demain* un vol pour ...?** ākelār ēyätēl ōzhōōrdvē/dəmeN eN vōl pōōr ...?
When will we be in ...?	**A quelle heure arrive-t-on à ...?** ākelār ärēvtôN ä ...?
How much will it cost to fly to ... (round trip)?	**Combien coûte un vol (aller-retour) pour ...?** kôNbyeN kōōt eN vōl (älā-rətōōr) pōōr ...?
I'd like a ticket to ..., ...	**Un billet pour ..., s'il vous plaît.** eN bēye pōōr ..., sēl vōō ple.

? **Aller simple ou aller-retour?** älä seNp'le ōō älä-rətōōr? | One way or round trip?

? **Classe économie, classe affaires ou première classe?** kläs ākônômē, kläs äfer ōō prəmyer kläs? | Economy, business or first class?

! **Ce vol est malheureusement complet.** sə vôl e mälārāzmäN kôNple. | I'm afraid this flight is sold out.

Are there any *special rates/stand-by seats* available?	**Est-ce qu'il y a des *tarifs spéciaux/ places stand by?*** eskēlyä dā tārēf spāsyō/pläs stäNd-bä'ē?

3

| I'd like ... | **Je voudrais une place ...** |
| | zhə vōōdre ĕn pläs ... |

a window seat.	**fenêtre.** fənet'rə.
an aisle seat.	**couloir.** kōōlô·är.
a seat in nonsmoking.	**non-fumeurs.** nôN-fēmār.
a seat in smoking.	**fumeurs.** fēmār.

| Where is Gate B? | **Où est la sortie B?** ōō e lä sôrtē bā? |

| I'd like to ... my flight. | **Je voudrais ... mon vol.** |
| | zhə vōōdre ... môN vôl. |

confirm	**faire confirmer** fer kôNfērmā
cancel	**annuler** änēlā
change	**modifier** môdēfyā

On the Plane

| Could I have *(another/ some more)* ..., please? | **Est-ce que je peux avoir (encore) ..., s'il vous plaît?** eskə zhə pā ävô·är (äNkôr) ..., sēl vōō ple? |

| I feel sick. | **J'ai mal au cœur.** zhā mäl ō kār. |

| Do you have something for air sickness? | **Est-ce que vous avez un remède contre le mal de l'air?** eskə vōōzävā eN rəmed kôNtrə lə mäl də ler? |

air sickness bag	**le sachet vomitoire** lə säshe vômētô·är
airline	**la compagnie aérienne**
	lä kôNpänyē ä·ārē·en
airplane	**l'avion** *m* lävyôN
airport	**l'aéroport** *m* lä·ārōpôr
arrival	**l'arrivée** *f* lärēvā
to book	**réserver** rāzervā
to cancel	**annuler** änēlā
to change	**modifier** môdēfyā
charter flight	**le vol charter** lə vôl shärter
class	**la classe** lä kläs
to confirm	**confirmer** kôNfērmā
counter	**le guichet** lə gēshe
delay	**le retard** lə rətär
departure	**le départ** lə dāpär
desk	**le guichet** lə gēshe
exit	**la sortie** lä sôrtē
flight	**le vol** lə vôl
– attendant *(male)*	**le steward** lə styōō·ärd
– attendant *(female)*	**l'hôtesse** *f* **de l'air** lōtes də ler
to fly	**voler** vôlā
carry-on luggage	**les bagages** *m/pl* **à main**
	lā bägäzh ä meN
information desk	**le guichet d'information**
	lə gēshe deNfôrmäsyôN
local time	**l'heure** *f* **locale** lār lôkäl

nonsmoking	**le non-fumeur** lə nôN-fēmär
return flight	**le vol de retour** lə vôl də rətōōr
scheduled flight	**le vol de ligne** lə vôl də lēn'yə
smoking	**le fumeur** lə fēmär
stopover	**l'escale** *f* leskäl
ticket	**le billet** lə bēye

RAIL

Information and Tickets

At which station can I get a train to ...?

Pour aller à ..., je dois partir de quelle gare? pōōr älä ä ..., zhə dô·ä pärtēr də kel gär?

Where is the *train/ tourist* information office?

Où *sont les renseignements/est l'office du tourisme?* ōō sôN lā ränNsen'yəmäN/ e lôfēs də tōōrēsm?

Where can I find the *luggage storage/ lockers*?

Où est la *consigne/consigne automatique?* ōō e lä kôNsēn'yə/ kôNsēnyôtômätēk?

When is the *next/last* train to ...?

A quelle heure part le *prochain/dernier* train pour ...? äkelər pär lə prôsheN/dernyā treN pōōr ...?

When will it arrive in ...?

A quelle heure arrive-t-il à ...? äkelər ärēvtēl ä ...?

When are the trains to ...?

Quand y a-t-il des trains pour ...? käN yätēl dā treN pōōr ...?

Do I have to change trains?	**Est-ce que je dois changer?**
	eskə zhə dô·ä shäNzhā?
Which platform does the train to ... leave from?	**De quel quai part le train pour ...?**
	də kel kā pär lə treN pōōr ...?
How much does a ticket to ... cost?	**Combien coûte un billet pour ...?**
	kôNbyeN kōōt eN bēye pōōr ...?
Are there special rates for ...?	**Est-ce qu'il y a des réductions pour ...?** eskēlyä dā rädēksyôN pōōr ...?
Do you have to pay extra for this train?	**Est-ce que ce train est à supplément?**
	eskə sə treN etä sēplämäN?
I'd like *a ticket/two tickets* to ..., ... please.	**Un billet/Deux billets pour ..., s'il vous plaît, ...** eN bēye/dœ bēye pōōr ..., sēl vōō ple ...
first/second class	*première/deuxième* classe.
	prəmyer/dœzyem kläs.
for children	**pour enfants.** pōōr äNfäN.
for adults	**pour adultes.** pōōr ädœlt.

3

| **?** | **Aller simple ou aller-retour?** | One way or round |
| | älā seNp'lə ōō älā-rətōōr? | trip? |

| I'd like to reserve a seat on the ... o'clock train to ..., please. | **Réservez-moi une place dans le train de ... heures pour ..., s'il vous plaît.** |
| | rāzervā-mô·ä œn pläs däN lə treN də ... ær pōōr ..., sēl vōō ple. |

65

? **Compartiment ou voiture salle?** Compartment or open
kôNpärtēmäN ōō vô·ätēr säl? seating?

I'd like a seat ... **J'aimerais avoir une place ...**
zhāmərə ävô·är ēn pläs ...

by the window.	**fenêtre.** fənet'rə.	
in nonsmoking.	**non-fumeurs.** nôN-fēmār.	
in smoking.	**fumeurs.** fēmār.	

INFO In France you must stamp your ticket at one of the
machines (**composteurs**) standing at the entrance
to the platforms before you begin your journey.

Information

Accès aux quais äkse ō kā	To All Trains
Consigne kôNsēn'yə	Baggage Storage
Consigne automatique kôNsēnyôtômätēk	Lockers
Enregistrement des bagages äNrzhēstrəmäN dā bägäzh	Baggage Check-In
Lavabos läväbō	Washrooms
Renseignements räNsenyəmäN	Information
Restaurant de la gare restôräN də lä gär	Restaurant
Salle d'attente säl dätäNt	Waiting Room
Sortie sôrtē	Exit
Toilettes tô·älet	Rest Rooms
Voie vô·ä	Track

On the Train

May I sit here?	**Est-ce que cette place est libre?**
	eskə set pläs e lēb'rə?

Excuse me, but I believe this is my seat.	**Excusez-moi, c'est ma place.**
	ekskēzā-mô·ä, se mä pläs.

Would you mind if I *opened/closed* the window?	**Vous permettez que *j'ouvre/je ferme* la fenêtre?** vōō permetā kə *zhōōv'rə)/ferm* lä fənet'rə?

!	**Les billets, s'il vous plaît!** lā bēye, sēl vōō ple!	Tickets, please!

How many more stops to ...?	**Combien y a-t-il encore d'arrêts jusqu'à ...?** kôNbyeN yätēl äNkôr däre zhēskä ...?

How long is our layover?	**Combien de temps dure l'arrêt?** kôNbyeN də täN dēr läre?

Will I be in time to catch the train to ...?	**Est-ce que j'aurai le train de ...?** eskə zhôrā lə treN də ...?

Train

arrival	**l'arrivée** *f* lärēvā
car	**la voiture, le wagon** lä vô·ätēr, lə vägôN
to change (trains)	**changer de train** shäNzhā də treN
class	**la classe** lä kläs
compartment	**le compartiment** lə kôNpärtēmäN
connection	**la correspondance** lä kôrespôNdäNs
departure	**le départ** lə dāpär

dining car	**le wagon-restaurant**
	lə vägôN-restôräN
discount	**la réduction** lä rädēksyôN
exit	**la sortie** lä sôrtē
extra cost	**le supplément** lə sēplämäN
family compartment	**le compartiment «Espace-enfants»**
	lə kôNpärtēmäN espäs-äNfäN
fare	**le prix du billet** lə prē dē bēye
to get off	**descendre** dāsäNd'rə
to get on	**monter** môNtä
platform	**le quai** lə kā
reserved	**réservé** räzervā
seat	**la place** lä pläs
sleeper *(many beds)*	**la voiture-couchettes**
	lä vô·ätēr-kōōshet
sleeper *(1–4 beds)*	**le wagon-lit** lə vägôN-lē
stop	**l'arrêt** *m* läre
taken	**occupé** ôkēpā
through car	**la voiture directe** lä vô·ätēr dērekt
ticket	**le billet** lə bēye
timetable	**l'horaire** *m* lôrer
track	**la voie** lä vô·ä
train	**le train** lə treN
– station	**la gare** lä gär

BOAT

Information and Booking

When will there be a *ship/ferry* going to ...? | **Quand y a-t-il un** *bateau/ferry* **pour ...?** käN yätēl eN bätō/ferē pōōr

How long is the passage to ...? | **Combien de temps dure la traversée pour ...?** kôNbyeN də täN dēr lä träversä pōōr ...?

When must we be on board? | **Quand devons-nous être à bord?** käN dəvôN-nōō eträ bôr?

I'd like to board with a car. | **Je voudrais embarquer une voiture.** zhə vōōdre äNbärkā ēn vô-ätēr.

I'd like a *first class/ tourist class* ticket to ... | **Je voudrais un billet de bateau** *pre- mière classe/classe touriste* **pour ...** zhə vōōdre eN bēye də bätō prəmyer kläs/kläs tōōrēst pōōr ...

I'd like a ticket for the excursion at ... o'clock. | **Je voudrais un billet pour l'excursion de ... heures.** zhə vōōdre eN bēye pōōr lekskērsyôN də ... ēr.

Where has the ... docked? | **Où est accosté le ...?** ōō etäkôstā lə ...?

On Board

I'm looking for cabin number ...	**Je cherche la cabine numéro ...** zhə shersh lä käbēn nēmārō ...
May I have a different cabin?	**Est-ce que je pourrais changer de cabine?** eskə zhə pōōre shäNzhā də käbēn?
Do you have something for sea-sickness?	**Vous avez un remède contre le mal de mer?** vōōzävā eN rəmed kôNt'rə lə mäl də mer?

Boat

air conditioning	**l'air** *m* **conditionné** ler kôNdēsyônā
blanket	**la couverture** lä kōōvertēr
boat-trip	**la croisière** lä krô-äzyer
cabin	**la cabine** lä käbēn
canal	**le canal** lə känäl
captain	**le capitaine** lə käpēten
car ferry	**le car-ferry** lə kär-ferē
coast	**la côte** lä kōt
deck	**le pont** lə pôN
dining hall	**la salle à manger** lə säl ä mäNzhā
double cabin	**la cabine double** lä käbēn dōōb'lə
drawbridge	**le pont levant** lə pôN ləväN
exterior cabin	**la cabine extérieure** lä käbēn ekstäryēr
ferry	**le ferry** lə ferē
four-bed cabin	**la cabine à quatre personnes** lä käbēn ä kät'rə persôn

70

hovercraft	**l'hydroglisseur** *m* lēdrōglēsǘr
interior cabin	**la cabine intérieure** lä käbēn eNtǟryǘr
island	**l'île** *f* lēl
land excursion	**l'excursion** *f* **à terre** lekskērsyôN ä ter
landing	**le point d'accostage** lə pô·eN däkôstäzh
lifeboat	**l'embarcation** *f* **de sauvetage** läNbärkäsyôN də sōvtäzh
life vest	**le gilet de sauvetage** lə zhēle də sōvtäzh
lock	**l'écluse** *f* läklēz ·
lounge chair	**la chaise longue** lä shez lôNg
passage	**la traversée** lä trävĕrsā
port	**le port** lə pôr
rough sea	**la mer agitée** lä mer äzhētā
sea	**la mer** lä mer
sea-sickness	**le mal de mer** lə mäl də mer
ship	**le bateau** lə bätō
ship's agent	**l'agence** *f* **maritime** läzhäNs märētēm
shore	**le rivage** lə rēväzh
single cabin	**la cabine individuelle** lä käbēn eNdēvēdē·el
steward	**le steward** lə styōō·ärd
sun deck	**le sundeck** lə sǟndek
swimming pool	**la piscine** lä pēsēn
trip	**l'excursion** *f* lekskērsyôN

CAR, MOTORBIKE AND BIKE

Rentals

I'd like to rent a ... (with automatic transmission).

Je voudrais louer ... (avec changement de vitesses automatique). zhe vōōdre lōō-ā ... (ävek shäNzhmäN de vētes ôtômätēk).

car	**une voiture** ēn vô·ätēr	
four-wheel drive	**un 4x4** eN kät're kät're	
van	**un minibus** eN mēnēbēs	
motorcycle	**une moto** ēn mōtō	
motor home	**un camping-car** eN käNpēng-kär	

INFO The RN (**route nationale**) is comparable to an interstate road, the RD (**route départementale**) to a state road.

You may drive up to 50 km/hour (30 mph) within towns, up to 90 km/hour (55 mph) on state roads without a center stripe, and up to 110 km/hour (65 mph) on state roads with a passing lane or center stripe. You may accelerate up to 110 km/hour on the city highways and up to 130 km/hour (75 mph) on the other French national highways.

? **Est-ce que je pourrais voir votre permis de conduire (international)?** eske zhe pōōre vô·är vôt're permē de kôNdē·ēr (eNternäsyônäl)?

May I see your (international) driver's license, please?

I'd like to rent a *bicycle/mountain bike* (with back-pedal brakes).	**Je voudrais louer** *une bicyclette/un V.T.T.* **(avec rétropédalage).** zhə vōōdre lōō-ā ēn bēsēklet/eN vā-tā-tā (ävek rātrôpädäläz).
I'd like to rent it (for) ...	**Je voudrais louer la voiture pour ...** zhə vōōdre lōō-ā lä vô·ätēr pōōr ...
tomorrow.	**demain.** dəmeN.
the day after tomorrow.	**après-demain.** äpre-dəmeN.
one day.	**une journée.** ēn zhōōrnā.
one week.	**une semaine.** ēn səmen.

?	**Quelle sorte de voiture désirez-vous?** kel sôrt də vô·ätēr dāzērā-vōō?	What kind of car would you like?

How much does it cost?	**Combien ça coûte?** kôNbyeN sä kōōt?
How much mileage is included in the price?	**Combien de kilomètres sont inclus dans le prix?** kôNbyeN də kēlômet'rə sôNteNklē dāN lə prē?

INFO French national highways are toll roads. You must pay the toll at the (automatic) toll booths **(péage (automatique).** Before you drive up you will see signs that say **"Péage. Préparez votre monnaie."** – "Toll approaching. Please have exact change ready." If you don't have the exact amount, drive into the lane marked **"Usagers sans monnaie"** – "Drivers without exact change."

What kind of fuel does it take?	**Quelle sorte de carburant est-ce-qu'elle consomme?** kel sôrt də kárb**ē**räN eskel kôNsôm?
Is comprehensive insurance included?	**L'assurance tous risques est comprise?** läs**ē**räNs tōō r**ē**sk e kôNpr**ē**z?
How much is the deductible?	**A combien s'élève la franchise?** ä kôNbyeN s**ā**lev lä fräNsh**ē**z?
Can I return the car in ...?	**Je peux aussi restituer la voiture à ...?** zhə p**ā** ôs**ē** rest**ē**t**ē**ā-lä vô-ät**ē**r ä ...?
When do I have to be back?	**A quelle heure est-ce que je dois être de retour?** äkel**ā**r eskə zhə dô-ä et'rə də rətōōr?
I'd also like a helmet.	**Donnez-moi aussi un casque de protection, s'il vous plaît.** dônā-mô-ä ôs**ē** eN käsk də prôteksyôN, s**ē**l vōō ple.

Parking

| Is there a parking *garage/lot* nearby? | **Est-ce qu'il y a un *parking couvert/ parking* par ici?** esk**ē**lyä eN párk**ē**ng kōōvär/párk**ē**ng pär **ē**s**ē**? |
| Is the parking lot supervised? | **Est-ce que le parking est gardé?** eskə lə pärk**ē**ng e gärd**ā**? |

INFO In France there is often a limit to the length of time you may leave your car parked somewhere. Frequently you must get a parking receipt from one of the parking timer machines: **"Prenez un ticket à l'horodateur."**

Is the parking garage open all night?	**Est-ce que le parking est ouvert toute la nuit?** eskə lə pärkēng etōōver tōōt lä nē·ē?
Can I park here?	**Je peux me garer ici?** zhə pā mə gärā ēsē?

Gas Stations, Car Repair

Where is/How far is it to the nearest gas station?	**Où/A quelle distance se trouve la station-service la plus proche?** ōō/ä kel dēstäNs sə trōōv lä stäsyôN-servēs lä plē prôsh?
... euros' worth of ..., please.	**Pour ... euros ..., s'il vous plaît.** pōōr ... ārō' ..., sēl vōō ple.
unleaded	**d'ordinaire sans plomb** dôrdēnār säN plôN
diesel	**de gazole** də gäzôl
leaded	**d'ordinaire** dôrdēnār
super unleaded	**de super sans plomb** də sēpär säN plôN
super leaded	**de super avec plomb** də sēpär ävek plôN
two-stroke engine fuel	**de mélange deux-temps** də mäläNzh də̲-täN.

| Fill it up, please. | **Le plein, s'il vous plaît.** |
| | lə pleN, sēl vōō plā. |

| I'd like *1 liter/2 liters* of oil, please. | **Je voudrais *1 litre/2 litres* d'huile.** |
| | zhe vōōdre *eN lēt'rə/dā lēt'rə* dē·ēl. |

| Could you change the oil, please? | **Une vidange, s'il vous plaît.** |
| | ēN vēdäNzh, sēl vōō ple. |

| I need snow chains. | **Il me faudrait des chaînes (à neige).** |
| | ēl mə fōdre dā shen (ä nezh). |

Breakdown and Accidents

| Please call ..., quickly! | **Vite, appelez ...** vēt, äplā ... |

the fire department	**les pompiers!** lā pôNpyā!
an ambulance	**une ambulance!** ēn äNbēläNs!
the police	**la police!** lā pôlēs!

| I've had an accident. | **J'ai eu un accident.** |
| | zhā ē enäksēdäN. |

| May I use your phone? | **Je peux téléphoner de chez vous?** |
| | zhe pā tālāfônā də shā vōō? |

| Nobody's hurt. | **Personne n'est blessé.** |
| | persôn ne blesā. |

| ... people have been (seriously) injured. | **Il y a ... blessés (graves).** |
| | ēlyä ... blesā (gräv). |

| Please help me. | **Aidez-moi, s'il vous plaît.** |
| | ādā-mô·ä, sēl vōō ple. |

| I need some bandages. | **J'ai besoin de pansements.** |
| | zhā bezô·eN də päNsmäN. |

| I'm out of gas. | **Je suis en panne sèche.** |
| | zhə svē äN pän sesh. |

| The radiator's over-heating. | **L'eau du radiateur bout.** |
| | lō dē rädyätēr bōō. |

| Could you ... | **Est-ce que vous pourriez ...** |
| | eskə vōō pōōryā ... |

| give me a lift? | **m'emmener un bout de chemin?** |
| | mämnā eN bōō də shəmeN? |

| tow my car? | **remorquer ma voiture?** |
| | rəmôrkä mä vô·ätēr? |

| send me a tow-truck? | **m'envoyer la dépanneuse?** |
| | mäNvô·äyā lä dāpänēz? |

| It's not my fault. | **Ce n'est pas de ma faute.** |
| | sə ne pä də mä fōt. |

| I think we should get the police. | **Je voudrais que l'on appelle la police.** |
| | zhə vōōdre ke lônäpel lä pôlēs. |

| I was doing ... kilometers an hour. | **Je faisais du ... zhə fəze dē ...** |

3

77

INFO One does not usually get in touch with the police after a minor "fender bender" accident in France. It is sufficient for both parties to fill out and sign an accident form (**constat à l'amiable**), complete with a sketch. If possible, include the names and addresses of any witnesses. Send this form to your insurance company; this does not signify acceptance of responsibility for the accident. If the parties involved cannot come to an agreement, however, then it would be advisable to call the police.

You didn't have the right-of-way.	**Vous n'avez pas respecté la priorité.** vōō nävä pä respektä lä prē-ôrētā.
You cut the corner.	**Vous avez coupé le virage.** vōōzävä kōōpä lə vēräzh.
You were following too closely.	**Vous m'avez collé.** vōō mävä kôlā.
You were going too fast.	**Vous rouliez trop vite.** vōō rōōlyä trō vēt.
You damaged the ...	**Vous avez endommagé ...** vōōzävä äNdômäzhā ...
May I have your name and address, please?	**Donnez-moi votre nom et votre adresse, s'il vous plaît.** dônā-mô·ä vôt'rə nôN ā vôträdres, sēl vōō ple.
May I have your insurance information, please?	**Donnez-moi le nom et le numéro de votre assurance, s'il vous plaît.** dônā-mô·ä lə nôN ā lə nēmārō də vôträsēērāNs, sēl vōō ple.

Here is my name and address.	**Voici mon nom et mon adresse.** vô·äsē môN nôN ā mônädres.
Here is my insurance information.	**Voici le nom et le numéro de mon assurance.** vô·äsē lə nôN ā lə nēmärō də mônäsēräNs.

! **Remplissez ce constat à l'amiable, s'il vous plaît.** räNplēsā sə kôNstä ä lämē·äb'lə, sēl vōō ple.	Would you fill out this accident form, please?

Would you mind being a witness?	**Vous pouvez servir de témoin?** vōō pōōvā servēr də tāmô·eN?

Do it yourself

Could you lend me ..., please?	**Vous pouvez me prêter ..., s'il vous plaît?** vōō pōōvā mə prätā ..., sēl vōō ple?

a bicycle repair kit	**un set de réparation pour vélo** eN set də räpäräsyôN pōōr vālō
a pump	**une pompe à air** ēn pôNp ä er
a ... wrench	**une clef anglaise (numéro ...)** ēn klä äNglez (nēmärō ...)
a screwdriver	**un tournevis** eN tōōrnəvēs
a ... socket wrench	**une clef à douille (numéro ...)** ēn klä ä dōō'ē (nēmärō ...)
a jack	**un cric** eN krēk
a tool kit	**des outils** dāzōōtē
a pair of pliers	**des pinces** dā peNs

At the Repair Shop

Where is the nearest garage/... -dealer's garage?	**Où est le garage/le concessionnaire le plus proche?** ōō e le gärázh/le kôNsesyôner le plē prôsh?
My car's (on the road to) ...	**Ma voiture se trouve (sur la route de)** ... mä vô-ätēr se trōōv (sēr lä rōōt de)
Can you tow it away?	**Vous pouvez la remorquer?** vōō pōōvā lä remôrkā?
Would you come with me?	**Vous pouvez venir avec moi?** vōō pōōvā venēr ävek mô-ä?
Would you have a look at it?	**Vous pourriez regarder, s'il vous plaît?** vōō pōōryā regärdā, sēl vōō ple?
... is broken.	**... est cassé.** ... e käsā.
My car won't start.	**Ma voiture ne démarre pas.** mä vô-ätēr ne dāmär pä.
The battery is dead.	**La batterie est vide.** lä bätrē e vēd.
The engine *sounds funny/doesn't have any power*.	**Le moteur *fait un bruit bizarre/ne tire pas*.** le môtēr fe eN brē-ē bēzär/ne tēr pä.
Just do the essential repairs, please.	**Ne faites que les réparations strictement nécessaires.** ne fet ke lā räpäräsyôN strēktemäN nāseser.

| Can I still drive it? | **Est-ce que je peux encore rouler avec?** eskə zhə pā äNkôr rōōlä ävek? |

| When will it be ready? | **Elle sera prête quand?** el sərä pret käN? |

Car, Motorbike and Bike

to accelerate	**accélérer** äksālārā
accelerator	**l'accélérateur** *m* läksälärätār
accident	**l'accident** *m* läksēdäN
– report	**le constat à l'amiable** lə kôNstä ä lämē·äb'lə
air conditioning	**la climatisation** lä klēmätēzäsyôN
air filter	**le filtre à air** lə fēlträler
ambulance	**l'ambulance** *f* läNbēläNs
antifreeze	**l'antigel** *m* läNtēzhel
automatic transmission	**le changement de vitesses automatique** lə shäNzhmäN də vētes ôtômätēk
battery	**la batterie** lä bätrē
bicycle	**la bicyclette** lä bēsēklet
brake	**le frein** lə freN
– fluid	**le liquide de freins** lə lēkēd də freN
– light	**les feux** *m/pl* **de stop** lā fā də stôp
broken	**cassé** käsā
bumper	**le pare-chocs** lə pär-shôk
car	**la voiture** lä vô·ätər

3

81

carburetor	**le carburateur** lə kärbērätār
catalytic converter	**le pot catalytique** lə pô kätälētēk
to change	**changer** shäNzhā
– gears	**passer une vitesse**
	päsā ēn vētes
child seat	**le siège pour enfant**
	lə syezh pōōr äNfäN
clutch	**l'embrayage** *m* läNbreyäzh
curve	**le virage** lə vēräzh
dealer's garage	**le concessionnaire** lə kôNsesyôner
distilled water	**l'eau** *f* **distillée** lō dēstēlā
to drive	**rouler** rōōlā
driver's license	**le permis de conduire**
	lə permē də kôNdē̱-ēr
dynamo	**la dynamo** lä dēnämō
emergency brake	**le frein à main** lə freN ä meN
engine	**le moteur** lə môtər
exhaust	**le pot d'échappement** lə pô dāshäpmäN
fan belt	**la courroie** lä kōōrô·ä
fender	**l'aile** *f* lel
first-aid kit	**la boîte de premiers secours**
	lä bô·ät də prəmyā səkōōr
four-wheel drive	**le 4x4** lə kät'rə kät'rə
fuse	**le fusible** lə fēsēb'lə
garage	**l'atelier** *m* **de réparation**
	lätəlyā də rāpäräsyôN
gas	**l'essence** *f* lesäNs
– station	**la station-service**
	lä stäsyôN-servēs

82

gear	**la vitesse** lä vētes
headlights	**le phare** lə fär
helmet	**le casque** lə käsk
high beams	**les feux** *m/pl* **de route** lä fā də rōōt
highway	**l'autoroute** *f* lôtôrōōt
horn	**le klaxon** lə kläksôN
hubcap	**l'enjoliveur** *m* läNzhôlēvär
ignition	**l'allumage** *m* lälēmäzh
– cable	**le fil d'allumage** lə fēl dälēmäzh
injured	**blessé** blesā
innertube	**la chambre à air** lä shäNbräler
insurance	**l'assurance** *f* läsēräNs
interstate road	**la route nationale** lä rōōt näsyônäl
joint	**le joint** lə zhô·eN
kilometer	**le kilomètre** lə kelômet'rə
low beams	**les feux** *m/pl* **de croisement** lä fā də krô·äzmäN
mirror	**le miroir** lə mērô·är
motor home	**le camping-car** lə käNpēng-kär
motorcycle	**la moto** lä mōtō
neutral	**le point mort** lə pô·eN môr
oil	**l'huile** *f* **moteur** lē·ēl môtär
– change	**la vidange** lə vēdäNzh
to park	**se garer** sə gärä
parking garage	**le parking couvert** lə pärkēng kōōver
parking light	**les feux de position** lä fā də pôzēsyôN
parking lot	**le parking** lə pärkēng
parking receipt machine	**l'horodateur** *m* lôrôdätär

3

83

pressure	**la pression des pneus**
	lä presyôN dā pnā
radiator	**le radiateur** lə rädē·ätār
rear-end collision	**le télescopage** lə tāleskôpäzh
registration number	**le numéro d'immatriculation**
	lə nēmārō dēmätrēkēl̄äsyôN
to rent	**louer** lōō·ā
repair	**la réparation** lä räpäräsyôN
to repair	**réparer** räpärā
right of way	**la priorité** lä prē·ôrētā
seatbelt	**la ceinture f de sécurité**
	lä seNtēr də säkērētä
shock absorbers	**l'amortisseur m** lämôrtēsār
spark plug	**la bougie** lä bōōzhē
snow chains	**les chaînes f/pl à neige**
	lā shen ä nezh
spare gas canister	**le bidon de secours**
	lə bēdôN də səkōōr
spare part	**la pièce de rechange**
	lä pyes də rəshäNzh
spare tire	**le pneu de secours** lə pnā də səkōōr
starter	**le démarreur** lə dāmärār
state road	**la route secondaire** lä rōōt səkôNder
steering	**la direction** lä dēreksyôN
taillight	**les feux m/pl arrière** lā fā äryer
tire	**le pneu** lə pnā
toll	**le péage** lə pā·äzh
– booth	**le péage** lə pā·äzh

84

– road	**la section à péage**
	lä seksyôN ä pā·äzh
to tow (away)	**remorquer** rəmôrkā
tow rope	**le câble de remorquage**
	lə käb'lə də rəmôrkäzh
transmission	**la boîte de vitesses** lä bô·ät də vētes
turn indicator	**le clignotant** lə klēnyôtäN
unleaded	**sans plomb** säN plôN
valve	**la soupape** lä sōōpäp
van	**le minibus** lə mēnēbēs
vehicle registration	**la carte grise** lä kärt grēz
warning sign	**le triangle de signalisation**
	lə trē·äNg'lə də sēnyälēzäsyôN
water	**l'eau** *f* lō
wheel	**la roue** lä rōōt
windshield wiper	**les balais** *m/pl* **d'essuie-glaces**
blades	lā bäle desē·ē-gläs
witness	**le témoin** lə tāmô·eN

3

85

BUS, SUBWAY, TAXI

By Bus and Subway

Where's the nearest subway station?	**Où est la station de métro la plus proche?** ōō e lä stäsyôN də mätrō lä plẽ prôsh?
Where's *bus/streetcar* stop for ...?	**Où se trouve l'arrêt du *bus/tramway* pour ...?** ōō sə trōōv läre dẽ *bēs/trämōō-e* pōōr ...?
Which *bus/subway* goes to ...?	**Quel *bus/métro* va à ...?** kel *bēs/mätrō* vä ä ...?

! **La ligne ...** lä lēn'yə ...   Number...

When is the next *bus/ streetcar* to ...?	**A quelle heure part le prochain *bus/ tramway* pour ...?** äkelär pär lə prôsheN *bēs/trämōō-e* pōōr ...?
When does the last *bus/subway* return?	**A quelle heure revient le dernier *bus/ métro*?** äkelär rəvyeN lə dernyā *bēs/mätrō*?
Does this *bus/subway* go to ...?	**Est-ce que ce *bus/métro* va à ...?** eskə sə *bēs/mätrō* vä ä ...?
Do I have to transfer to get to ...?	**Pour ..., est-ce que je dois changer?** pōōr ..., eskə zhə dô-ä shäNzhā?
Could you tell me where I have to *get off/transfer*, please?	**Pouvez-vous me dire où je dois *descendre/changer*?** pōōvä-vōō mə dēr ōō zhə dô-ä *däsäNd'rə/shäNzhā*?

INFO You can obtain bus tickets at bus stations or major bus stops; otherwise you can purchase them from the bus driver. Don't forget to stamp them in the machine on the bus, otherwise they are not valid.

You can buy tickets for the subway and commuter trains at the window in front of the entrance. In Paris, as well as some other big cities, you can obtain a general ticket for the entire transportation system or for certain parts of it. In addition there are also special tickets for tourists that include the entrance fees to museums, such as the ticket **Paris-Visite**.

Rather than buy individual tickets, it is advisable to purchase a **carnet** (a book of 10 tickets). When you enter the **métro** (subway), you must put your card through the barrier in order to get in. Your ticket is then valid within the **métro** system until you leave it.

Where can I get a ticket?	**Où est-ce qu'on peut acheter les tickets?** ōō eskôN pā āshtā lā tēke?
Are there ...	**Il y a ...** ēlyä ...
day passes?	**des tickets pour la journée?** dā tēke pōōr lä zhōōrnä?
weekly tickets?	**des cartes hebdomadaires?** dā kärt ebdômäder?
books of tickets?	**des carnets?** dā kärne?
I'd like a ticket to ..., please.	**Un ticket pour ..., s'il vous plaît.** eN tēke pōōr ..., sēl vōō ple.

Taxi!

Where can I get a taxi?	**Où est-ce que je peux avoir un taxi?** ō eskə zhə pā ävô·är eN täksē?
Could you order a taxi for me for tomorrow morning at ... o'clock?	**Vous pourriez me commander un taxi pour demain matin à ... heures?** vōō pōōryā mə kômäNdä eN täksē pōōr dəmeN mäteN ä ... ār?
..., please.	**..., s'il vous plaît.** sēl vōō ple.
To the train station	**À la gare** ä lä gär
To the airport	**À l'aéroport** ä lä·ārōpôr
To the ... Hotel	**À l'hôtel ...** ä lōtel ...
How much is it to ...?	**Combien ce sera pour aller à ...?** kôNbyeN sə sərä pōōr älä ä ...?
(In the hotel) I was told it would only cost ... francs.	**On m'a dit (à l'hôtel) que ça ne coûte que ... francs.** ôN mä dē (ä lōtel) kə sä nə kōōt kə ... fräN.
Would you _start/reset_ the taxometer, please?	**Mettez votre compteur _en marche/sur zéro_, s'il vous plaît.** metā vôt'rə kôNtār äN märsh/sēr zärō, sēl vōō ple.
Could you _wait/stop_ here (for a moment), please?	**_Attendez/Arrêtez-vous_ (un instant) ici, s'il vous plaît.** ätäNdā/ärätā-vōō (eNeNstäN) ēsē, sēl vōō ple.

88

Bus, Subway, Taxi

bus	**le bus** lə bēs
– stop	**l'arrêt** *m* **de bus** läre də bēs
– terminal	**la gare routière** lä gär rōōtyer
to change	**changer** shäNzha
commuter train	**le RER** lə er-ə-er
day pass	**le ticket pour la journée** lə tēke pōōr lä zhōōrnä
departure	**le départ** lə dāpär
direction	**la direction** lä dēreksyôN
driver	**le chauffeur** lə shôfȧr
to get out	**descendre** dāsäNd'rə
last stop	**le terminus** lə termēnēs
receipt	**le reçu** lə rəsē
schedule	**l'horaire** *m* lôrer
to stamp (a ticket)	**composter** kôNpôstā
stop	**l'arrêt** *m* läre
streetcar	**le tramway** lə trämōō-e
subway	**le métro** lə mātrō
taxi	**le taxi** lə täksē
– stand	**la station de taxis** lä stäsyôN də täksē
ticket	**le ticket** lə tēke
– (vending) machine	**le distributeur automatique de tickets** lə dēstrēbȧtār ôtômätēk də tēke
weekly ticket	**la carte hebdomadaire** lä kärt ebdômäder

3

HITCHHIKING

I'd like to go to ...

Je voudrais aller à ... zhə vōōdre älä ä ...

Where/Which way are
you going?

Vous allez où? vōōzälā ōō?

Can you take me (a
part of the way) there?

**Vous pouvez m'emmener (un bout de
chemin)?** vōō pōōvā mämnā (eN
bōōdshəmeN)?

? Où voulez-vous descendre?
ōō vōōlā-vōō dāsäNd'rə?

Where do you want
to get off?

Could you let me out
here, please?

**Laissez-moi descendre ici, s'il vous
plaît.** lesā-mô·ä dāsäNdrēsē, sēl vōō
ple.

Thanks for the lift.

Merci beaucoup de m'avoir emmené.
mersē bōkōō də mävô·är ämnā.

Food and Drink

MENU MENU

Potages et soupes *Soups*

bouillabaisse *f* bōōyäbes	(southern French) fish soup
consommé *m* kôNsômā	consommé
potage *m* **parmentier** pôtäzh pärmäNtyā	potato soup
soupe *f* **à l'oignon** sōōp ä lônyôN	French onion soup
soupe *f* **de poisson** sōōp də pô·äsôN	fish soup

Hors-d'œuvre *Appetizers*

avocat *m* **vinaigrette** ävôkä vēnegret	avocados in vinaigrette
charcuterie *f* shärkētrē	cold cut platter
cœurs *m/pl* **d'artichauts** kär därtēshō	artichoke hearts
crudités *f/pl* **(variées)** krēdētā (väryā)	crudités (fresh, raw vegetable platter as finger food)
huîtres *f/pl* ē·ēt'rə	oysters
olives *f/pl* ôlēv	olives
pâté *m* pätā	(liver) pâté
– **de campagne** də käNpän'yə	coarse (liver) pâté
pissenlits *m/pl* **au lard** pēsäNlē ō lär	dandelion green salad with bacon
rillettes (de tours) *f/pl* rēyet (də tōōr)	(pork) pâté

92

salade *f* sälåd

  – **composée** kôNpôzā

  – **mixte** mēkst

  – **niçoise** nēsô·äz

saumon *m* **fumé** sōmôN fēmā

terrine *f* **de canard**
terēn də känär

salad

  chef salad

  mixed salad

  green salad with eggs, tomatoes, sardines, olives, and capers

smoked salmon

duck pâté

Entrées Starters

bouchées *f/pl* **à la reine**
bōōshā ä lä ren

crêpes *f/pl* krep

croque-monsieur *m*
krôk-məsyā

escargots *m/pl* eskärgō

omelette *f* **aux champignons**
ômlet ō shäNpēnyôN

quiche *f* **lorraine** kēsh lôren

tarte *f* **à l'oignon** tärt ä lônyôN

vol au vents

crêpes

toasted ham-and-cheese sandwich

snails

mushroom omelette

quiche lorraine (bacon and cheese quiche)

onion tart

Viandes Meat dishes

agneau *m* änyō

bœuf *m* bāf

lièvre *m* lēyev'rə

mouton *m* mōōtôN

lamb

beef

hare

mutton

4

porc *m* pôr

pork

veau *m* vō

veal

andouillette *f* äNdōoyet

tripe sausage

bifteck *m* bēftek

steak

bœuf *m* **bourguignon**

beef in red wine

bǣf bōōrgēnyôN

bœuf *m* **à la mode** bǣf ä lä

pot roast

môd

boudin *m* bōōdeN

blood sausage

cassoulet *m* käsōōle

casserole of navy beans, goose, and other meats

côte *f* kōt

chop

escalope *f* **de veau**

veal cutlet

eskälôp də vō

filet *m* **de bœuf** fēle də bǣf

filet of beef

gigot *m* **d'agneau** zhēgō dänyō

leg of lamb

grillade *f* grēyäd

grilled meat platter

hachis *m* äshē

meat loaf

jarret *m* **de veau** zhäre də vō

knuckle of veal

quenelles *f/pl* kənel

meat or fish dumplings

ris *m* **de veau** rē də vō

veal sweetbreads

rôti *m* rōtē

roast

sauté *m* **de veau** sôtē də vō

veal stew

selle *f* **d'agneau** sel dänyō

rack of lamb

steak *m* stek

steak

　　– au poivre ō pô·äv'rə

pepper –

　　– haché äshā

Salisbury –

tournedos *m* tōōrnədō

fillet steak

tripes *f/pl* trēp

tripe

Volaille   *Poultry*

blanc *m* **de poulet**   chicken breast
bläN də pōōle

canard *m* **à l'orange**   duck with orange sauce
känär ä lôräNzh

confit *m* **de canard**   duck preserved in its own fat
kôNfē də känär

coq *m* **au vin** kôkōveN   chicken in wine sauce

dinde *f* deNd   turkey

pintade *f* peNtäd   guinea fowl

poulet *m* **rôti** pōōle rōtē   roast chicken

Poissons   *Fish*

aiglefin *m* āgləfeN   haddock

anguille *f* äNgē'yə   eel

brochet *m* brôshe   pike

cabillaud *m* käbēyō   cod

calmar *m* **frit** kälmär frē   deep-fried squid

carpe *f* kärp   carp

colin *m* kôleN   hake

friture *f* frētēr   mixed deep-fried fish

lotte *f* lôt   monkfish

morue *f* môrē   dried cod

rouget *m* rōōzhe   perch

saumon *m* sōmôN   salmon

sole *f* sôl   sole

thon *m* tôN   tuna

truite *f* **au bleu** trē̄-ēt ō blǟ   poached trout

95

Coquillages et crustacés *Seafood*

coquilles *f/pl* **Saint-Jacques** scallops
kôkē'yə seN-zhäk

crabes *m/pl* kräb crabs

crevettes *f/pl* krəvet shrimps

écrevisses *f/pl* ākrəvēs freshwater crawfishes

huîtres *f/pl* ē-ēt'rə oysters

langouste *f* läNgōōst crawfish, spiny lobster

langoustines *f/pl* läNgōōstēn Dublin bay prawns

moules *f/pl* mōōl mussels

plateau *m* **de fruits de mer** seafood platter
plätō də frē̄-ē də mer

Légumes *Vegetables*

artichauts *m/pl* ärtēshō artichokes

asperges *f/pl* äsperzh asparagus

aubergines *f/pl* ōberzhēn eggplants

carottes *f/pl* kärôt carrots

champignons *m/pl* mushrooms
shäNpēnyôN

chou *m* shōō cabbage
   – de Bruxelles də brēsel   Brussels sprouts
   – -fleur flār   cauliflower
   – rouge rōōzh   red cabbage

choucroute *f* shōōkrōōt sauerkraut

courgettes *f/pl* kōōrzhet zucchinis

épinards *m/pl* āpēnär spinach

endives *f/pl* äNdēv Belgian endive

fenouil *m* fənōō'ē	fennel
haricots *m/pl* ärēkō	beans
macédoine *f* **de légumes**	mixed vegetables
mäsädō·än də lāgēm	
navets *m/pl* näve	turnips
petits pois *m/pl* pətē pô·ä	peas
poivron *m* pô·ävrôN	bell pepper
ratatouille *f* rätätōō'ē	vegetable stew of tomatoes, peppers, zucchini, and eggplant

Comment le désirez-vous? How would you like it?

bien cuit byeN kē·ē	well done
(fait) maison (fe) mäzôN	homemade
farci färsē	stuffed
fumé fēmā	smoked
gratiné grätēnā	au gratin
rôti rōtē	roasted

Garnitures Vegetables and side dishes

gratin *m* **dauphinois**	potatoes au gratin
gräteN dōfēnô·ä	
pâtes *f/pl* pät	pasta
pommes *f/pl* **de terre**	potatoes
pôm də ter	
– **frites** frēt	French fries
– **sautées** sōtā	fried potatoes
riz *m* rē	rice

4

97

Fromages *Cheese*

bleu *m* blȳ
fromage *m* frômäzh
  – au lait cru ō le krȳ

  – de brebis də brəbē
  – de chèvre də shev'rə
plateau *m* **de fromages**
plätō də frômäzh

blue cheese
cheese
  cheese made from un-
  pasteurized milk
  feta cheese
  goat's cheese
cheese platter

Desserts *Desserts*

beignets *m/pl* **aux pommes**
benye ō pôm
coupe *f* **maison**
kōōp mezôN
crème *f* **caramel**
krem kärämel
flan *m* fläN
glace *f* gläs
  – à la fraise ä lä frez
  – à la vanille ä lä vänē'yə
  – au chocolat ō shôkôlä
île *f* **flottante** ēl flôtäNt
macédoine *f* **de fruits**
mäsädô·än də frȳ·ē
meringue *f* məreNg
parfait *m* pärfe

fried apple rings

house ice-cream sundae

crème caramel

baked egg custard
ice cream
  strawberry –
  vanilla –
  chocolate –
ice-cream on vanilla sauce
fruit salad

meringue
ice-cream parfait

Fruits   Fruit

fraises *f/pl* frez — strawberries
framboises *f/pl* fräNbô·äz — raspberries
melon *m* məlôN — melon
pastèque *f* pästek — watermelon
pêche *f* pesh — peach
poire *f* pô·är — pear
pomme *f* pôm — apple
raisins *m/pl* rezeN — grapes

Gâteaux et pâtisseries   Cake

biscuit *m* **roulé** — Swiss roll
bēskē̇·ē rōōlā
cake *m* kek — fruit cake
chausson *m* **aux pommes** — apple Danish
shôsôN ō pôm
chou *m* **à la crème** — cream puff
shōō ä lä krem
éclair *m* äkler — éclair
  – au café ō käfā — coffee –
mille-feuille *m* mēl-fa̤'ē — napoleon
profiteroles *f/pl* prôfētərôl — small cream puffs
tarte *f* tärt — tart
  – aux pommes ō pôm — apple –
  – Tatin täteN — caramelized apple –
tartelette *f* **aux fraises** — small strawberry tarts
tärtəlet ō frez

4

99

BOISSONS BEVERAGES

Apéritifs *aperitifs*

kir *m* kēr — kir
porto *m* pôrtō — port
pastis *m* pästēs — anise liqueur

Vins *Wine*

vin *m* veN — wine
– **blanc** bläN — white –
– **rouge** rōōzh — red –
– **rosé** rōzā — rosé
– **d'appellation contrôlée** — vintage –
  däpeläsyôN kôNtrôlā
– **mousseux** mōōsā — sparkling –
champagne *m* shäNpän'yə — champagne
brut brē — dry
(demi-)sec (dəmē) sek — (medium) dry
doux dōō — sweet

Autres boissons alcoolisées *Other alcoholic drinks*

bière *f* byer — beer
– **sans alcool** säN älkôl — nonalcoholic –
– **brune** brēn — ale
– **blonde** blôNd — lager
– **pression** presyôN — draft beer
bitter *m* bēter — bitters

calvados *m* kälvädôs	applejack
cassis *m* käsēs	red-currant liqueur
digestif *m* dēzhestēf	digestive schnapps

Boissons non alcoolisées *Non-alcoholic drinks*

citron *m* pressé sētrôN presā	freshly squeezed lemon juice
eau *f* minérale ō mēnäräl	mineral water
– gazeuse gäzēz	carbonated –
– non gazeuse nôN gäzēz	noncarbonated –
jus *m* zhē	juice
– de pomme də pôm	apple –
– d'orange dôräNzh	orange –
– de tomate de tômät	tomato –
limonade *f* lēmônäd	(fizzy) lemonade
menthe *f* mäNt	peppermint syrup with mineral water

Boissons chaudes *Hot drinks*

café *m* käfā	coffee
– express ekspres	espresso
– au lait ō le	– with hot milk
– crème krem	– with frothed milk
chocolat *m* chaud shôkôlä shō	hot chocolate
infusion *f* eNfēzyôN	herbal tea
thé *m* tā	tea
– au citron ō sētrôN	– with lemon

4

INFORMATION

Where is ... around here?	**Où y a-t-il ici ...** ōō yätēl ...

a good restaurant	**un bon restaurant?** eN bôN restôräN?
an inexpensive restaurant	**un restaurant pas trop cher?** eN restôräN pä trō sher?
a restaurant typical for this area	**un restaurant typique?** eN restôräN tēpēk?
a bar	**un bistrot?** eN bēstrō?
a café	**un salon de thé?** eN sälôN də tā?

INFO One visits the **café** primarily to get something to drink; they might also have sandwiches there, **croque-monsieur** (toasted ham and cheese) or **croque-madame** (toasted ham and cheese with pineapple). In the morning you can also get a French breakfast there.

In the **café-bar** there might only be a few tables. Most people will be standing at the bar. If cigarettes are also sold there, it will be called a **café-bar-tabac**, indicated by a large, red cigar hanging on the door.

In the **café-restaurant** you can get something to drink and/or eat. The service and decor are unembellished, the food and drink inexpensive.

A **bistro** is a smaller café, usually with an interesting atmosphere. In Paris you can sample different wines at the **bistros à vin**. They usually also offer a few (regional) dishes such as **steak**, **bœuf bourguignon**, etc., so that you don't have to drink on an empty stomach.

A table for ..., please.	**Une table pour ... personnes, s'il vous plaît.** ēn täb'lə pōōr ... persôn, sēl vōō ple.

May I have this seat?	**Est-ce que cette place est libre?** eske set pläs e lēb'rə?

INFO At the **café** you may sit down where there is space available, even at tables where other people are sitting. This is not a good idea at a **restaurant**: you should wait until you are shown to a table.

Do you have a high-chair?	**Avez-vous une chaise haute pour enfants?** ävā-vōō ēn shez ōt pōōr äNfäN?

Excuse me, where are the restrooms?	**Pardon, où sont les toilettes?** pärdôN, ōō sôN lā tô·älet?

! **Par ici.** pär ēsē.   Down here.

WAITER!

May I see a menu, please?	**La carte, s'il vous plaît.** lä kärt, sēl vōō ple.

INFO In France you can call the waiter by saying **Monsieur** məsyā, and call the waitress by saying **Madame** mädäm or **Mademoiselle** mädmô·äzel.

4

I'd like something to eat.	**Je voudrais manger.** zhə vōōdre mäNzhā.
I'd just like something small to eat.	**Je voudrais seulement manger un petit quelque chose.** zhə vōōdre sälmäN mäNzhā eN pətē kelkə shōz.
Are you still serving hot meals?	**Est-ce qu'on peut encore avoir quelque chose de chaud à manger?** eskôN pā äNkôr ävô·är kelkə shōz də shō ä mäNzhā?
I just want something to drink.	**Je voudrais seulement boire quelque chose.** zhə vōōdre sälmäN bô·är kelkə shōz.

? **Que désirez-vous boire?**
kə dāzērā-vōō bô·är?

What would you like to drink?

I'd like ..., please.	**Je voudrais ...** zhə vōōdre ...
a quarter of a liter of red wine.	**un quart de vin rouge.** eN kär də veN rōōzh.
a carafe of water	**une carafe d'eau.** ēn käräf dō.
a bottle of mineral water	**une bouteille d'eau minérale.** ēn bōōte'ē dō mēnäräl.
Can I get a carafe of wine?	**Avez-vous aussi du vin en carafe?** ävā-vōō ôsē dē veN äN käräf?

? **Que désirez-vous manger?**
kə dāzerā-vōō mäNzhā?

What would you like to eat?

I'd like ...	**Je voudrais ...** zhə vōōdre ...
the meal for ... francs.	**le menu à ... francs.** lə mənē̠ ä ... fräN.
a serving of ...	**une portion de ...** ēn pôrsyôN də ...

Do you have ...?	**Avez-vous ...?** ävā-vōō ...?

What would you recommend?	**Que me recommandez-vous?** kə mə rəkômäNdā-vōō?

> **!** **Je vous recommande ...** I can recommend ...
> zhə vōō rəkômäNd ...

What is the special of the day?	**Quel est le plat du jour?** kel e lə plä dē̠ zhōōr?

What are the local specialties?	**Quelles sont les spécialités de la région?** kel sôN lā späsyälētā də lä räzhē-ôN?

Do you have children's portions?	**Avez-vous un menu enfants?** ävä-vōō eN mənē̠ äNfäN?

Do you have ...	**Avez-vous ...** ävä-vōō ...
vegetarian dishes?	**de la cuisine végétarienne?** də lä kē̠-ēzēn väzhätäryen?
food suitable for diabetics?	**des plats pour diabétiques?** dā plä pōōr dē-äbätēk?
special diet meals?	**des plats de régime?** dā plä də räzhēm?

4

105

Does that have … in it? I'm not allowed to eat that.	**Est-ce qu'il y a … dans ce plat? Je n'ai pas le droit d'en manger.** eskēlyä … däN sə plá? zhə ne pä lə drô·ä däN mäNzhä.

Is there garlic in that?	**Est-ce qu'il y a de l'ail dedans?** eskēlyä də lä'ē dədäN?

?	**Comme *entrée/dessert*, qu'est-ce que vous prenez?** kôm äNtrā/ dāser, keskə vōō prənā?	What would you like for *an appetizer/ dessert?*

Thanks, but I'd rather not have *an appetizer/ any dessert.*	**Merci, je ne prends pas *d'entrée/de dessert.*** mersē, zhə nə präN pä däNtrā/də dāser.

INFO The French end a good meal with a **plateau de fromages** plätō də frômäzh (cheese platter). There are usually 4 to 5 kinds of cheese on the platter; however, it is considered impolite to sample more than 2 or 3 of them.

Could I have … instead of …?	**Est-ce que je pourrais avoir … au lieu de …?** eskə zhə pōōre ävô·är … ō lēyä də …?

Could you bring me another …, please?	**Apportez moi encore …, s'il vous plaît.** äpôrtā mô·ä äNkôr …, sēl vōō ple.

INFO Bread – **pain** – is included in the price of meals, and French waiters customarily refill the bread basket as soon as it is empty.

	Comment désirez-vous votre steak? kômäN dāzērā-vōō vôt'rə stek?	How would you like your steak?

Rare. | **Saignant.** senyäN.

Medium. | **A point.** ä pô·eN.

Well done. | **Bien cuit.** byeN kē·ē.

INFO In a restaurant you will usually get a complementary carafe of water for your table. Many people in France, however, have begun drinking mineral water, with the result that waiters do not always automatically bring plain water to the tables. Do not hesitate to ask for **une carafe d'eau** ēn käräf dō (a pitcher of water).

COMPLAINTS

I didn't order this. I wanted ... | **Ce n'est pas ce que j'ai commandé. Je voulais ...** sə ne pä səkə zhā kômäNdā. zhə vōōle ...

The ... *is/are* missing. | **Ici, il manque encore ...** ēsē, ēl mäNk äNkôr ...

The food is ... | **C'est ...** se ...

    cold. | **trop froid.** trō frô·ä..

    too salty. | **trop salé.** trō sälā.

    too greasy. | **trop gras.** trō grä..

4

| This is no longer fresh. | **Ce n'est plus très frais.** |
| | sə ne plē̠ tre fre. |

| The meat hasn't been cooked enough. | **La viande n'est pas assez cuite.** |
| | lä vyäNd ne päzäsā kē̠·ēt. |

| Would you take it back, please? | **Remportez cela, s'il vous plaît.** |
| | räNpôrtā səlä, sēl vōō ple. |

THE CHECK, PLEASE.

? **Vous êtes satisfaits?**
vōōzet sätēsfe?

Did you enjoy your meal?

| It was very nice, thank you. | **Merci, c'était très bon.** |
| | mersē̠, säte tre bôN. |

| Could I have the check, please? | **L'addition, s'il vous plaît.** |
| | lädēsyôN, sēl vōō ple. |

| I'd like a receipt. | **Je voudrais une facture.** |
| | zhə vōōdre ēn fäktē̠r. |

INFO Waiters will not continually visit your table to ask if you want anything else or if everything is all right. They will also not bring the check when you have finished your meal until you ask for it. If you wish to have separate checks, you must tell the waiter that **"Nous voudrions payer séparément"** nōō vōōdrēôN päyā säpärämäN. The check will be brought discreetly on a small plate.

| May I treat you? | **Je peux t'inviter?** zhə pā̠ teNvētā? |

You're my guest today.	**Aujourd'hui, c'est moi qui vous invite.** ōzhōōrdvē, se mô-ä kē vōōzeNvēt.
I think there must be some mistake here.	**A mon avis, il y a une erreur.** ä mônävē, ēlyä ēn erär.
Will you please add it up again?	**Vous pourriez me refaire le compte, s'il vous plaît?** vōō pōōryä mə rəfer lə kôNt, sēl vōō ple?
We didn't order this.	**Nous n'avions pas commandé cela.** nōō nävyôN pä kômäNdä səlä.
Thank you very much.	**Merci beaucoup.** mersē bōkōō.

DINING WITH FRIENDS

Enjoy your meal!	**Bon appétit!** bônäpätē!
Your health!	**A votre/ta santé!** ä vôt'rə/tä säNtä!
Cheers!	**Tchin-tchin!** tshēn-tshēn!

? *Vous aimez/tu aimes ça?* vōōzāmā/tē em sä? How do you like it? **4**

It's very good, thank you.	**Merci, c'est très bon.** mersē, se tre bôN.
That's absolutely delicious.	**C'est absolument délicieux.** setäbsôlēmäN dālēsyä.

? *Vous en voulez?/Tu en veux?* vōōzäN vōōlä?/tē äN vä? Would you like some of this?

! **C'est une spécialité française.**   This is a French spe-
   setē̞n spāsyälē̞tä fräNsez.   ciality.

? **Encore un peu de ...?**   Would you like some
   äNkôr eN pā̞ də ...?   more ...?

Yes, please.   **Oui, volontiers.** ōō-ē̞, vôlôNtyā.

No, thanks, I'm fine   **Pas pour l'instant, merci.**
for the moment.   pä pōōr leNstäN, mersē.

No, thank you, I'm   **Je n'ai plus faim, merci.**
full.   zhə ne plē̞ feN, mersē.

What's that?   **Qu'est-ce que c'est?** keskə se?

INFO If you order **un café** in a **café**, you will receive a
small cup of coffee without milk. You can also get
un café crème, or **un crème** for short, which is a cup of coffee
with frothy milk. If you would like a large cup, ask for **un grand
crème**.

Would you pass me   *Vous pourriez/Tu pourrais* me passer
the ..., please?   ..., s'il *vous/te* plaît? vōō pōōryā/tē̞
   pōōre mə päsä ..., sēl vōō/tə ple?

Do you mind if I   **Ça *vous/te* dérange si je fume?**
smoke?   sä vōō/tə däräNzh sē zhə fē̞m?

Thank you for inviting   **Merci pour l'invitation.**
me/us.   mersē pōōr leNvē̞täsyôN.

It was wonderful.   **C'était excellent.** sāte ekseläN.

➦   *Please; Thank you (p.26)*

Food and drink

alcohol	**l'alcool** *m* lälkôl
appetizer	**l'entrée** *f*, **le hors-d'œuvre** läNtrā, lə ôr-dⱥv'rə
artificial sweetener	**la saccharine** lä säkärēn
ashtray	**le cendrier** lə säNdrē·ā
available	**libre** lēb'rə
bar	**le bistrot** lə bēstrō
beer	**la bière** lä byär
bottle	**la bouteille** lä bōōte'ē
bread	**le pain** lə peN
– roll	**le petit pain** lə pətē peN
white –	**le pain blanc** lə peN bläN
breakfast	**le petit déjeuner** lə pətē dāzhᾱnā
to bring	**apporter** äpôrtā
butter	**le beurre** lə bᾱr
cake	**le gâteau** lə gätō
carafe	**la carafe** lä käräf
chair	**la chaise** lä shez
chamomile tea	**la camomille** lä kämōmē'yə
cheese	**le fromage** lə frômäzh
cocoa	**le cacao** lə käkä·ō
coffee	**le café** lə käfā
black –	**le café noir** lə käfā nô·är
decaffeinated –	**le café décaféiné** lə käfā dākäfā·ēnā
– with hot milk	**le café au lait** lə käfā ō le
cold	**froid** frô·ä
– cuts	**la charcuterie** lä shärkētrē

4

111

cream	**la chantilly** lä shäNtēyē
crisp bread	**le pain croustillant** lə peN krōōstēyäN
cup	**la tasse** lä täs
dessert	**le dessert** lə däser
diabetic *(person)*	**le diabétique** lə dē-ábätēk
diabetic *(special food)*	**diabétique** dē-ábätēk
diet	**le régime** lə rāzhēm
dinner	**le dîner** lə dēnā
dish	**le plat** *m* lə plä
drink	**la boisson** lä bô-äsôN
to drink	**boire** bô-är
drinks menu	**la carte des boissons** lä kärt dā bô-äsôN
to eat	**manger** mäNzhā
egg	**l'œuf** *m, pl:* **les œufs** lạf, *pl:* lāzạ
fried –	**l'œuf** *m* **au plat** lạf ō plä
hard-boiled –	**l'œuf** *m* **dur** lạf dẹr
scrambled –	**l'œuf** *m* **brouillé** lạf brōōyā
soft-boiled –	**l'œuf** *m* **à la coque** lạf ä lä kôk
excellent	**excellent** ekseläN
fat	**le gras** lə grä
fatty	**gras** grä
fish	**le poisson** lə pô-äsôN
fork	**la fourchette** lä fōōrshet
fresh	**frais,** *f:* **fraîche** fre, *f:* fresh
fresh, raw vegetable platter *(finger food)*	**les crudités** *f/pl* lā krēdētā

112

fruit	**les fruits** *m/pl* lā frē·ē
to be full	**ne plus avoir faim** nə plēzävô·är feN
garlic	**l'ail** *m* lä'ē
glass	**le verre** lə ver
grease	**le gras** lə grä
greasy	**gras** grä
ham	**le jambon** lə zhäNbôN
hamburger	**le hamburger**
	lə äNbērgär
hard	**dur** dēr
to have breakfast	**prendre le petit déjeuner**
	präNd'rə lə pətē dāzhānā
herbs	**les fines herbes** *f/pl* lā fēn erb
homemade	**(fait) maison** (fe) mezôN
honey	**le miel** lə myel
hot *(temperature)*	**chaud** shō
hot *(spicy)*	**épicé** āpēsā
to be hungry	**avoir faim** ävô·är feN
ice (cube)	**le glaçon** lə gläsôN
ice cream	**la glace** lā gläs
to invite	**inviter** eNvētā
jam	**la confiture** lā kôNfētēr
ketchup	**le ketchup** lə ketshäp
knife	**le couteau** lə kōōtō
lean	**maigre** meg'rə
light food	**la cuisine diététique**
	lā kē·ēzēn dē·ātātēk
lunch	**le déjeuner** lə dāzhānā

4

main course	**le plat de résistance** lə plä də räzēstäNs
margarine	**la margarine** lä märgårēn
mayonnaise	**la mayonnaise** lä mäyônez
meal	**le repas** lə rəpä
meat	**la viande** lä vyäNd
menu	**la carte** lä kärt
milk	**le lait** lə le
mineral water	**l'eau _f_ minérale** lō mēnäräl
carbonated –	**l'eau _f_ gazeuse** lō gäzäz
non-carbonated –	**l'eau _f_ plate** lō plät
mushrooms	**les champignons** _m/pl_ lä shäNpēnyôN
mustard	**la moutarde** lä mōōtärd
napkin	**la serviette** lä servyet
non-alcoholic	**sans alcool** säNsälkôl
oil	**l'huile _f_** lē̜-ēl
olive –	**l'huile _f_ d'olive** lē̜-ēl dôlēv
onion	**l'oignon _m_** lônyôN
order	**la commande** lä kômäNd
to order	**commander** kômäNdā
pastries	**les gâteaux** _m/pl_ **secs** lä gätō sek
to pay	**payer** pāyā
pepper	**le poivre** lə pô-äv'rə
peppermint tea	**l'infusion _f_ de menthe** leNfē̜zyôN də mäNt
piece	**le morceau** lə môrsō
pizza	**la pizza** lä pētsä
place setting	**le couvert** lə kōōver
plate	**l'assiette _f_** läsyet

portion	**la portion** lä pôrsyôN
pumpernickel	**le pain bis** lə peN bē
to reserve	**réserver** räzervä
restaurant	**le restaurant** lə restôräN
rest room	**les toilettes** *f/pl* lā tô·älet
salad	**la salade** lä säläd
salt	**le sel** lə sel
sandwich	**le sandwich** lə säNdōō-ē(t)sh
sauce	**la sauce** lä sōs
seasoned	**assaisonné** äsesônā
seat	**la place** lä pläs
service	**le service** lə servēs
set menu	**le menu** lə mənē
slice	**la tranche** lä träNsh
soft	**tendre** täNd'rə
soup	**le potage** lə pôtäzh
sour	**aigre** āg'rə
special of the day	**le plat du jour** lə plä dē zhōōr
speciality	**la spécialité** lä späsyälētā
spice	**l'épice** *f* lāpēs
spoon	**la cuillère** lä kē·eyer
straw *(for drinks)*	**la paille** lä pä'yə
sugar	**le sucre** lə sēk'rə
sweet	**sucré** sēkrā
table	**la table** lä täb'lə
tea	**le thé** lə tā
fruit –	**l'infusion** *f* **fruitée** leNfēzyôN frē·ētā
herbal –	**l'infusion** *f* leNfēzyôN

4

to be thirsty	**avoir soif** ăvô·ār sô·äf
tip	**le pourboire** lə pōōrbô·ār
toast	**le toast** lə tōst
vegetables	**les légumes** *m/pl* lā lāgēm
vegetarian	**végétarien** vāzhātäryeN
vinegar	**le vinaigre** lə vēnāg'rə
waiter	**le garçon** lə gärsôN
waitress	**la serveuse** lä servāz
water	**l'eau** *f* lō
wine	**le vin** lə veN
zwieback	**les biscottes** *f/pl* lā bēskôt

 Food (p. 142)

Sightseeing

INFORMATION

Where is the tourist-information office?

Où se trouve l'office du tourisme?
ōō sə trōōv lôfēs dē tōōrēsm?

May I have ...

Je voudrais ... zhə vōōdre ...

a list of hotels?

une liste des hôtels.
ēn lēst dāzōtel.

a map of the area?

un plan des environs.
eN pläN dāzäNvērôN.

a street map?

un plan de la ville.
eN pläN də lä vēl.

a subway schedule?

un plan du métro.
eN pläN dē mātrō.

a schedule of events?

un calendrier des manifestations.
eN käläNdrē-ā dā mänēfestäsyôN.

Do you have any brochures in English?

Est-ce que vous avez aussi des prospectus en anglais? eskə vōōzävā ôsē dā prôspektēs änäNgle?

Could you reserve a room for me?

Est-ce que vous pouvez me réserver une chambre? eskə vōō pōōvā mə rāzervā ēn shäNb'rə?

INFO In many areas and cities popular with tourists, you will find a **petit train touristique**, a little train with open cars that travels through the streets instead of on tracks. Points of interest will be announced over the loudspeaker.

118

Are there *sightseeing tours/guided walking tours* of the city?	**Est-ce qu'il y a des *tours de ville guidés/visites guidées de la ville*?** eskēlyä dā *tōōr də vēl gēdä/vēzēt gēdä də lä vēl*?
How much does the sightseeing tour cost?	**Combien coûte le tour de ville guidé?** kôNbyeN kōōt lə tōōr də vēl gēdä?
How long does the walking tour last?	**Combien de temps dure la visite guidée de la ville?** kôNbyeN də täN dēr lä vēzēt gēdä də lä vēl?
I'd like *a ticket/two tickets* for the sightseeing tour, please.	**Un billet/Deux billets, s'il vous plaît, pour le tour de ville guidé.** eN bēye/dā bēye, sēl vōō ple, pōōr lə tōōr de vēl gēdä.

INFO In Paris you can take a trip on the **bateaux-mouches** and see the city from these sightseeing boats on the Seine. They dock at Pont Neuf, Pont de l'Alma, and the Pont d'Iéna under the Eiffel Tower.

I'd like to visit ...	**Je voudrais visiter ...** zhə vōōdre vēzētä ...
When is ... open?	**Quelles sont les heures d'ouverture de ...?** kel sôN lāzœr dōōvertēr də ...?

5

Please reserve a place/two places on tomorrow's excursion for me/us.	**Une place/Deux places pour l'excursion de demain à ..., s'il vous plaît.** ēn pläs/dā pläs poōr lekskērsyōN də dəmeN ä ..., sēl voō ple.
Where/When do we meet?	**Quand/Où est-ce que nous nous rencontrons?** käN/oō eskə noō noō räNkôNtrôN?
Is lunch included in the price?	**Est-ce que le déjeuner est inclus dans le prix?** eskə lə dāzhānā eteNklē däN lə prē?
Will we also be visiting ...?	**Est-ce que nous allons aussi visiter ...?** eskə noōzälôN ôsē vēzētā ...?
Will we also have some free time?	**Est-ce que nous avons du temps libre à notre disposition?** eskə noōzävôN dē täN lēbrä nôt'rə dēspôzēsyôN?
When will it start?	**Nous partons à quelle heure?** noō pärtôN ä kelār?
When do we get back?	**Nous rentrons à quelle heure?** noō räNtrôN ä kelār?

➡ *Accommodation (p. 36), Bus, Subway, Taxi (p. 86), On the Way (p. 54)*

SIGHTSEEING, EXCURSIONS

When is ... open?	**Quelles sont les heures d'ouverture de ...?** kel sôN läzær dövertēr də ...?
How long is ... open?	**... ♂ est ouvert/♀ est ouverte jusqu'à quelle heure?** ... ♂ etōōver/♀ etōōvert zhēskä kelär?
What does it cost to get in?	**Combien coûte l'entrée?** kôNbyeN kōōt läNtrā?
How much does the guided tour cost?	**Combien coûte la visite guidée?** kônbyeN kōōt lä vēzēt gēdā?
Is there a discount for ...	**Est-ce qu'il y a des réductions pour ...** eskēlyä dā rādēksyôN pōōr ...
families?	**les familles?** lä fämē'ē?
groups?	**les groupes?** lä grōōp?
children?	**les enfants?** läzäNfäN?
senior citizens?	**les personnes du troisième âge?** lä persôn dē trô·äzyem äzh?
students?	**les étudiants?** läzātēdyäN?

? **Vous avez une pièce d'identité sur vous?** vōōzävä ēn pyes dēdäNtētä sēr vōō? | Do you have *some ID/your passport* with you?

Do you also have tours in English?	**Est-ce qu'il y a aussi des visites guidées en anglais?** eskēlyä ôsē dā vēzēt gēdā änäNgle?	**5**

When does the tour begin?	**A quelle heure commence la visite?**
	äkelär kômäNs lä vēzēt?

One ticket/Two tickets, please.	**Un billet/Deux billets, s'il vous plaît.**
	eN bēye/dā bēye, sēl vōō ple.

Two adults and two children, please.	**Deux adultes, deux enfants, s'il vous plaît.**
	dāzädēlt, dāzäNfäN, sēl vōō ple.

INFO If you are interested in learning about France's history in an entertaining manner, try to attend a performance of the **Spectacle Son et Lumière**, a narrated slide-show. These presentations are frequently displayed in the castles along the Loire.

Are you allowed to *take pictures/make a video?*	**Est-ce qu'on a le droit de *prendre des photos/filmer?***
	eskônä lə drô·ä də präNd'rə dā fōtō/fēlmä?

What *building/monument* is that?	**Qu'est-ce que c'est que *cet édifice/ce monument?***
	keskə se kə set ādēfēs/sə mônēmäN?

Do you have a *catalog/guide?*	**Vous avez un *catalogue/guide?***
	vōōzävā eN kätälôg/gēd?

Do you have a ... of that picture?	**Vous avez une reproduction de ce tableau en ...** vōōzävä ēn rəprôdēksyôN də sə täblō äN ...

poster	**poster?** pôster?
postcard	**carte postale?** kärt pôstäl?
slide	**diapositive?** dyäpôsētēv?

122

abbey	**l'abbaye** *f* läbāē
abstract	**abstrait** äbstre
altar	**l'autel** *m* lōtel
amphitheater	**l'amphithéâtre** *m* läNfētā·ät'rə
antique	**antique** äNtēk
aqueduct	**l'aqueduc** *m* läkdēk
arch	**l'arc** *m* lärk
archeological find	**les vestiges** *m/pl* **archéologiques** lā vestēzh ärkā·ôlôzhēk
archeology	**l'archéologie** *f* lärkā·ôlôzhē
architect	**l'architecte** *m, f* lärshētekt
architecture	**l'architecture** *f* lärshētektēr
arena	**les arènes** *f/pl* lāzären
art	**l'art** *m* lär
– collection	**la collection de peintures** lä kôleksyôN də peNtēr
artist	**l'artiste** *m, f* lärtēst
baroque	**baroque** bärôk
basilica	**la basilique** lä bäzēlēk
bell	**la cloche** lä klôsh
bird sanctuary	**la réserve ornithologique** lä rāzerv ôrnētôlôzhēk
botanical gardens	**le jardin botanique** lə zhärdeN bôtänēk
bridge	**le pont** le pôN
brochure	**le prospectus** lə prospektēs
building	**l'édifice** *m* lādēfēs
bust	**le buste** lə bēst

5

123

cable car	**le téléphérique** lə tālāfārēk
canyon	**les gorges** *f/pl* lā gôrzh
capital *(of a column)*	**le chapiteau** lə shäpētō
castle	**le château** lə shätō
catacombs	**les catacombes** *f/pl* lā kätäkôNb
catalog	**le catalogue** lə kätälôg
cathedral	**la cathédrale** lä kätädräl
Catholic	**catholique** kätôlēk
cave	**la grotte** lä grôt
ceiling	**le plafond** lə pläfôN
Celtic	**celtique** seltēk
cemetery	**le cimetière** lə sēmtyer
central nave	**la nef centrale** lä nef säNträl
century	**le siècle** lə syek'lə
ceramics	**la céramique** lä särämēk
chair lift	**le télésiège** lə tālāsyezh
chamber of commerce	**le syndicat d'initiative** lə seNdēkä dēnēsyätēv
chapel	**la chapelle** lä shäpel
chimes	**le carillon** lə kärēyôN
choir	**le chœur** lə kār
church	**l'église** *f* lāglēz
– service	**l'office** *m* **religieux** lôfēs rəlēzhyā
– steeple	**le clocher** lə klôshā
– windows	**les vitraux** *m/pl* lā vētrō
city	**la ville** lä vēl
city center	**le centre ville** lə säNt'rə vēl
– district	**le quartier** lə kärtyā
– gate	**la porte de la ville** lä pôrt də lä vēl

city hall	**l'hôtel** *m* **de ville** lōtel də vēl
– walls	**les remparts** *m/pl* lā räNpär
classicism	**le classicisme** lə kläsēsēsm
cloister	**le cloître** lə klô·ät'rə
closed	**fermé** fermā
coat-of-arms	**les armes** *f/pl* lāzärm
collection	**la collection** lä kôleksyôN
column	**la colonne** lä kôlôn
convent	**le couvent** lə kōōväN
copy	**la copie** lä kôpē
court, courtyard	**la cour** lä kōōr
cross	**la croix** lä krô·ä
crypt	**la crypte** lä krēpt
discoverer	**le découvreur** lə dākōōvrär
dolmen	**le dolmen** lə dôlmen
dome	**la coupole** lä kōōpôl
drawing	**le dessin** lə deseN
dune	**la dune** lä dēn
dynasty	**la dynastie** lä dēnästē
emperor	**l'empereur** *m* läNprär
empress	**l'impératrice** *f* leNpärätrēs
engraving	**la gravure** lä grävēr
era	**l'époque** *f* lāpôk
excavations	**les fouilles** *f/pl* lā fōō'ē
excursion	**l'excursion** *f* lekskērsyôN
– boat	**la vedette d'excursion** lä vədet deskskērsyôN
exhibition	**l'exposition** *f* lekspōzēsyôN

expressionism	**l'expressionnisme** *m* lekspresyônēsm
façade	**la façade** lä fäsäd
flea market	**le marché aux puces** lə märshā ō pēs
forest	**la forêt** lä fôre
– fire	**l'incendie** *m* **de forêt** leNsäNdē də fôre
fort	**le fort** lə fôr
fortress	**le château fort** lə shätō fôr
fountain	**la fontaine** lä fôNten
fresco	**la fresque** lä fresk
frieze	**la frise** lä frēz
gable	**le pignon** lə pēnyôN
Gallo-Roman	**gallo-romain** gälō-rômeN
garden	**le jardin** lə zhärdeN
gate	**la porte** lä pôrt
glass	**le verre** lə ver
Gothic	**gothique** gôtēk
hall	**la salle** lä säl
harbor	**le port** lə pôr
historical part of the city/town	**la vieille ville** lä vyey vēl
history	**l'histoire** *f* lēstô·är
house	**la maison** lä mezôN
Impressionism	**l'impressionnisme** *m* leNpresyônēsm
influence	**l'influence** *f* leNflē·äNs
inscription	**l'inscription** *f* leNskrēpsyôN
inventor	**l'inventeur** *m* leNväNtär

Jewish	**juif** zhē-ēf
king	**le roi** lə rô-ä
lake	**le lac** lə läk
landscape	**le paysage** lə pā-ēzäzh
list of hotels	**la liste des hôtels** lä lēst däzōtel
main entrance	**le portail** lə pôrtä'ē
to make a video	**filmer** fēlmā
map	**le plan** lə pläN
marble	**le marbre** lə märb'rə
market	**le marché** lə märshā
covered –	**les halles** *f/pl* lā äl
mausoleum	**le mausolée** lə mōsôlā
memorial	**le site commémoratif** lə sēt kômāmôrätēf
Middle Ages	**le Moyen-Âge** lə mô-äyenäzh
mill	**le moulin** lə mōōleN
minaret	**le minaret** lə mēnäre
model	**la maquette** lä mäket
modern	**moderne** môdern
monastery	**le monastère** lə mônäster
monument	**le monument** lə mónēmäN
mosaic	**la mosaïque** lä môzä-ēk
mosque	**la mosquée** lä môskā
mountains	**les montagnes** *f/pl* lā môNtän'yə
museum	**le musée** lə mēzā
Muslim	**le musulman** lə mēzēlmäN
narrated slide show	**le spectacle Son et Lumière** lə spektäk'lə sôN ā lēmyer
national park	**le parc national** lə pärk näsyônäl

5

127

nature park	**la réserve zoologique**
	lä räzerv zô·ôlôzhēk
nature preserve	**le site naturel protégé**
	lə sēt nätērel prôtäzhā
nave	**la nef** lä nef
Neoclassicism	**le néoclassicisme**
	lə nā·ôkläsēsēsm
open	**ouvert** ōōver
opera	**l'opéra** *m* lôpärä
original	**l'original** *m* lôrēzhēnäl
ornamentation	**les ornements** *m/pl* läzôrnəmäN
painter	**le peintre** lə peNt'rə
painting	**la peinture** lä peNtēr
palace	**le palais** lə päle
panorama	**le panorama** lə pänôrämä
park	**le parc** lə pärk
pass	**le col** lə kôl
pedestrian zone	**la zone piétonne** lä zōn pyätôn
photograph	**la photo** lä fōtō
to photograph	**prendre des photos**
	präNd'rə dā fōtō
picture	**le tableau** lə täblō
pilgrim	**le pèlerin** lə pelreN
pilgrimage	**le pèlerinage** lə pelrēnäzh
pillar	**le pilier** lə pēlyā
portal	**le portail** lə pôrtä'ē
portrait	**le portrait** lə pôrtre
poster	**l'affiche** *f* läfēsh
pottery	**la poterie** lä pôtrē

Protestant	**protestant** prôtestäN
queen	**la reine** lä ren
to reconstruct	**reconstituer** rəkôNstētē̄·ā
region	**la région** lä rāzhē·ôN
relief	**le relief** lə rəlyef
religion	**la religion** lä rəlēzhyôN
remains	**les vestiges** *m/pl* lā vestēzh
Renaissance	**la Renaissance** lä rənesäNs
reservoir	**le lac de barrage** lə läk də bäräzh
to restore	**restaurer** restôrā
river	**la rivière** lä rēvyer
Roman	**romain** rômeN
Romanesque	**l'art** *m* **roman** lär rômäN
Romans	**les Romains** *m/pl* lā rômeN
Romanticism	**le romantisme** lə rômäNtēsm
roof	**le toit** lə tô·ä
ruins	**les ruines** *f/pl* lā rē·ēn
sand	**le sable** lə säb'lə
-stone	**le grès** lə gre
sculptor	**le sculpteur** lə skēlptār
sculpture	**la sculpture** lä skēlptēr
sights	**les curiosités** *f/pl* lā kēryōzētā
slide	**la diapositive** lä dyäpōzētēv
square *(in town)*	**la place** lä pläs
stadium	**le stade** lə städ
stalactite cave	**la grotte à concrétions** lä grôt ä kôNkrāsyôN
statue	**la statue** lä stätē̄
still life	**la nature morte** lä nätēr môrt

5

street map	**le plan de la ville** lə pläN də lä vēl
stucco	**le stuc** lə stᴇk
style	**le style** lə stēl
surrounding area	**les environs** *m/pl* lāzäNvērôN
synagogue	**la synagogue** lä sēnägôg
tapestry	**la tapisserie** lä täpēsrē
temple	**le temple** lə täNp'lə
theater	**le théâtre** lə tā·ät'rə
tomb	**la tombe** lä tôNb
tour	**la visite** lä vēzēt
tourist guide	**le guide** lə gēd
tourist-information office	**l'office** *m* **du tourisme** lôfēs dᴇ tōōrēsm
tower	**la tour** lä tōōr
treasure chamber	**le trésor** lə trāzôr
valley	**la vallée** lä välā
vase	**le vase** lə väz
vault	**la voûte** lä vōōt
view	**la vue** lä vᴇ
vineyards	**les vignobles** *m/pl* lā vēnyôb'lə
to visit	**visiter** vēzētā
volcano	**le volcan** lə vôlkäN
wall	**le mur** lə mᴇr
waterfall	**la cascade** lä käskäd
window	**la fenêtre** lä fənet'rə
wine cellar	**le caveau à vin** lə kävō ä veN
wine tasting	**la dégustation de vin** lä dāgᴇstäsyôN də veN

wine-makers' guild	**la coopérative vinicole**
	lä kô-ôpārätēv vēnēkôl
winery	**la propriété vinicole**
	lä prôprē-ātā vēnēkôl
wing	**l'aile** *f* lel
wooden engraving	**la gravure sur bois** lä grävēr sēr bô·ä
work	**l'œuvre** *f* lǣv'rə
zoo	**le zoo** lə zô·ô

INFO There are many wildlife parks in France, some with exotic animals and some with animals in danger of extinction (e.g., eagles, wolves). One of the most famous is the **Réserve de loups des Cévennes**. In the Camargue, an 800 km² (app. 288 square miles) nature reserve in southern France, you will encounter a unique world of plants and animals. The Camargue is famous for its wild white horses, flamingos, and black bulls. In the Pyrenees there are still some bears living in the wild. And on the Côte d'Azur some cities – Antibes, for example – have dolphin aquariums.

5

Animals

bear	**l'ours** *m* lōōrs
bull	**le taureau** lə tôrō
dolphin	**le dauphin** lə dôfeN
eagle	**l'aigle** *m* leg'lə
horse	**le cheval** lə shəväl
lizard	**le lézard** lə lāzär
seagull	**la mouette** lä mōō·et
stork	**la cigogne** lä sēgôn'yə

Plants

broom	**le genêt** lə gene
century plant	**l'agave** *m* lägäv
cork oak	**le chêne-liège** lə shen-lyezh
cypress	**le cyprès** lə sēprē
eucalyptus tree	**l'eucalyptus** *m* lākälēptēs
fig tree	**le figuier** lə fēgyā
heather	**la bruyère** lä brēyer
holm (oak) tree	**le chêne vert** lə shen ver
lavender	**la lavande** lä läväNd
Mediterranean brushwood	**le maquis** lə mäkē
oak tree	**le chêne** lə shen
oleander	**le laurier-rose** lə lôryā-rōz
olive tree	**l'olivier** *m* lôlēvyā
orange tree	**l'oranger** *m* lôräNzhā
palm tree	**le palmier** lə pälmyā
pine tree	**le pin (maritime)** lə peN (märētēm)

132

Shopping

BASIC PHRASES

Where can I get ...? **Où est-ce que je peux acheter ...?**
ōō eskə zhə pā äshtā ...?

? Vous désirez? vōō dāzērā? May I help you?

? Est-ce que je peux vous aider? Can I help you with
eskə zhə pā vōōzādā? something?

Thanks, but I'm just **Merci, je regarde seulement.**
looking. mersē, zhə rəgärd sə̄lmäN.

Someone's already **Merci, on me sert.** mersē, ôN mə ser.
helping me, thanks.

I'd like ... **Je voudrais ...** zhə vōōdre ...

May I have ..., please? **Donnez-moi ..., s'il vous plaît.**
dónā-mô·à ..., sēl vōō ple.

a can of ...	**une boîte de ...** ēn bô·ät də ...
a bottle of ...	**une bouteille de ...** ēn bōōte'ē də ...
a jar of ...	**un pot de ...** eN pô də ...
a pack of ...	**un paquet de ...** eN päke də ...

! Je regrette, nous n'avons plus I'm sorry, but we
de ... zhə rəgret, nōō nävôN plē don't have any
də ... more ...

How much is/are ...? **Combien coûte/coûtent ...?**
kôNbyeN kōōt/kōōt ...?

| I don't really like that. | **Cela ne me plaît pas tellement.** |
| | sälä nə mə ple pä telmäN. |

| Could you show me something else? | **Vous pourriez me montrer autre chose?** vōō pōōryä mə môNtrā ōt'rə shōz? |

| Do you have anything less expensive? | **Vous n'auriez rien de moins cher?** vōō nôryä ryeN də mô·N sher? |

INFO Stores in France are generally open until 7 or 7:30 p.m.; smaller grocery stores may be open a bit longer. They are frequently closed at lunchtime from 12 p.m. to 2 p.m. Grocery stores, bakeries, and butchers might also be open on Sunday mornings, but most stores are closed on Monday mornings.

| I'll have to think about it. | **Je dois encore réfléchir.** zhə dô·ä äNkôr rāflāshēr. |

| I like this. I'll take it. | **Cela me plaît. Je le prends.** sälä mə ple. zhə lə präN. |

| **?** **Vous désirez encore quelque chose?** vōō dāzērā äNkôr kelkə shōz? | Will there be anything else? |

| That's all, thank you. | **Merci, ce sera tout.** mersē, sə sərä tōō. |

| Can I pay with this credit card? | **Est-ce que je peux payer avec cette carte de crédit?** eskə zhə pā pāyā ävek set kärt də krādē? |

135

May I have a bag for it?	**Vous auriez un sac en plastique?** vōōzôryä eN säk äN plästēk?
Could you wrap it, please?	**Vous pourriez me l'emballer?** vōō pōōryā mə läNbälä?
How much does that cost?	**Ça coûte combien?** sä kōōt kôNbyēN?
Would you give me a receipt, please?	**Vous pourriez me donner un reçu, s'il vous plaît?** vōō pōōryā mə dônā eN rəsē, sēl vōō ple?
This is broken. Do you think you could fix it?	**C'est cassé. Vous pouvez le réparer?** se käsā. vōō pōōvā lə räpärā?
When will it be ready?	**Ce sera prêt quand?** sə särä pre käN?
I'd like to *exchange/ return* this.	**Je voudrais *échanger/rendre* cela.** zhə vōōdre āshäNzhā/räNd'rə selä.
I'd like a refund, please.	**Je voudrais être remboursé.** zhə vōōdre et'rə räNbōōrsā.
Excuse me, but you haven't given me enough change. I'm short ...	**Vous ne m'avez pas assez rendu. Il manque ...** vōō nə mävā päzäsā räNdē. ēl mäNk ...

bag	**le sac** lə säk
better	**meilleur** meyər
big	**grand** gräN
bigger	**plus grand** plē gräN
bottle	**la bouteille** lä bōōte'ē
to buy	**acheter** äshtā
can	**la boîte** lä bô·ät
to cost	**coûter** kōōtä
check	**le chèque** lə shek
classic	**classique** kläsēk
credit card	**la carte de crédit** lä kärt də krädē
to exchange	**échanger** äshäNzhā
expensive	**cher** sher
to give	**donner** dônā
present	**le cadeau** lə kädō
heavy	**lourd** lōōr
jar	**le pot** lə pô
less expensive	**moins cher** mô·eN sher
light *(weight)*	**léger** lāzhā
modern	**moderne** môdern
money	**l'argent** *m* lärzhäN
more expensive	**plus cher** plē sher
narrow	**étroit** ātrô·ä
package	**le paquet** lə päke
receipt	**le reçu** lə rəsē
to return	**rendre** räNd(rə)
round	**rond** rôN
sale(s)	**les soldes** *f/pl* lä sôld

self-service	**le libre-service** lə lēb'rə-servēs
to sell	**vendre** väNd'rə
to serve	**servir** servēr
shop window	**la vitrine** lä vētrēn
to show	**montrer** môNtrā
small	**petit** pətē
smaller	**plus petit** plē pətē
soft	**mou** mōō
special offer	**l'article** *m* **en promotion** lärtēk'lə äN prômôsyôN
to take	**prendre** präNd'rə
thick	**épais** āpe
thin	**mince** meNs
too ...	**trop ...** trō ...
wide	**large** lärzh

INFO You can purchase only meat in the **boucherie**; sausages and ham are offered in the **charcuterie**. These stores are quite commonly combined into a **boucherie-charcuterie**, where you can get both. You can get prepared foods and appetizers in the **rôtisserie** and from the **traiteur**. Milk products are sold in the **crémerie**: **lait** (milk), **yaourt** (yogurt), **fromage blanc** (cream cheese), and a great many different kinds of cheese. In the **boulangerie** you can buy bread and baked goods as well as simple cakes. If you wish to purchase more elaborate cakes and tarts, visit the **pâtisserie**. By the way, the **magasin libre-service** is a self-service store, frequently a small supermarket.

138

Colors and Patterns

beige	**beige** bezh
black	**noir** nó·är
blue	**bleu** blā
brown	**marron** *(inv)* märôN
colorful	**multicolore** mēltēkôlôr
dark	**... foncé** ... fôNsā
gold(en)	**doré** dôrā
gray	**gris** grē
green	**vert** ver
light *(color)*	**... clair** ... kler
patterned	**imprimé** eNprēmā
pink	**rose** rōz
purple	**violet** vyôle
red	**rouge** rōōzh
silver	**argent** *(inv)* ärzhäN
solid *(of color)*	**uni** ēnē
striped	**rayé** rāyā
white	**blanc** bläN
yellow	**jaune** zhōn

INFO If you have rented a vacation home or are camping and will be catering for yourself, you will probably go shopping at the **supermarchés** (supermarkets) or **hypermarchés** (superstores). They are usually located on the outskirts of town so that you will probably need a car to get to them. You can get everything there. Tip: tank up your car there, too; gas is usually cheaper there than at a normal gas station.

Stores

antique shop	**le magasin d'antiquités, le brocanteur** le mägäzeN däNtēkētā, lə brókäNtär
baker	**la boulangerie** lä bōōläNzhrē
barber	**le coiffeur** lə kô·äfār
beauty shop	**salon de beauté** sälôN də bōtā
bookstore	**la librairie** lä lēbrerē
butcher's shop	**la boucherie** lä bōōshrē
camera store	**le magasin d'articles photographiques** lə mägäzeN därtēk'lə fōtōgräfēk
candy store	**la confiserie** lä kôNfēzrē
confectionery	**la pâtisserie** lä pätēsrē
dairy (store)	**la crémerie** lä kremrē
delicatessen	**l'épicerie f fine** läpēsrē fēn
delicatessen *(cold cuts etc.)*	**la charcuterie** lä shärkētrē
department store	**le grand magasin** lə gräN mägäzeN
dry cleaner's	**le pressing** lə presēng
drugstore	**la droguerie** lä drôgrē
electrician's	**le magasin d'électroménager** lə mägäzeN dälektrōmänäzhā
fish store	**la poissonnerie** lä pô·äsônrē
flower shop	**le fleuriste** lə flärēst
grocery store	**l'épicerie f** läpēsrē
hair dresser's	**le coiffeur** lə kô·äfār
jewelry store	**le bijoutier** lə bēzhōōtyā
laundromat	**la laverie automatique** lä lävrē ôtômätēk
leather-goods store	**la maroquinerie** lä märôkēnrē

140

music store	**le magasin de disques** lə mägäzeN də dēsk
newsstand	**le marchand de journaux, le kiosque** lə märshäN də zhōōrnō, lə kē·ôsk
optician's	**l'opticien** *m* lôptēsyeN
perfume store	**la parfumerie** lä pärfēmrē
shoe store	**le magasin de chaussures** lə mägäzeN də shôsēr
shoe-repair shop	**le cordonnier** lə kôrdônyā
shopping center	**le centre commercial** lə säNt'rə kômersyäl
souvenir store	**le magasin de souvenirs** lə mägäzeN də sōōvnēr
sporting-goods store	**le magasin d'articles de sport** lə mägäzeN därtēk'lə də spôr
supermarket	**le supermarché** lə sēpermärshā
tobacconist	**le bureau de tabac** lə bērō də täbä

6

INFO Particularly in the summer you might often see the sign **Brocante**, indicating one of the numerous second-hand markets or shops, where it might well be worthwhile to have a look around. The **magasin d'antiquités**, on the other hand, sells valuable antiques.

141

FOOD

What's that?	**Qu'est-ce que c'est?** keskə se?
Could I have ..., please?	**Donnez-moi ..., s'il vous plaît.** dônā-mô·ä ..., sēl vōō ple.
100 grams of ...	**cent grammes de ...** säN gräm də ...
a quarter of ...	**un quart de ...** eN kär də ...
(half) a pound of ...	**une (demi-)livre de ...** ēn (dəmē-)lēv'rə də ...
a kilo of ...	**un kilo de ...** eN kēlô də ...
a slice of ...	**une tranche de ...** ēn träNsh də ...
a piece of ...	**un morceau de ...** eN môrsō də ...
(half) a liter of ...	**un (demi-)litre de ...** eN (dəmē-)lēt'rə də ...
A little *less/more*, please.	**Un peu *moins/plus*, s'il vous plaît.** eN pə *mô·N/plēs*, sēl vōō ple.
May I try some (of that)?	**Je peux goûter (de ça)?** zhə pə gōōtā (də sä)?

Food

alcohol-free beer	**la bière sans alcool** lä byer säN älkôl
apple	**la pomme** lä pôm
– juice	**le jus de pomme** lə zhē də pôm
apricot	**l'abricot** *m* äbrēkō
artichoke	**l'artichaut** *m* lärtēshō
artificial sweetener	**la saccharine** lä säkärēn

142

avocado	**l'avocat** m lävôkä
baby food	**les aliments** m/pl **pour bébés** lāzälēmäN pōōr bäbä
banana	**la banane** lä bänän
basil	**le basilic** lə bäzēlēk
beans	**les haricots** m/pl lā ärēkō
beef	**le bœuf** lə bəf
beer	**la bière** lä byer
Belgian endive	**l'endive** f läNdēv
bread	**le pain** lə peN
white –	**le pain blanc** lə peN bläN
broccoli	**le brocoli** lə brôkôlē
butter	**le beurre** lə bər
cake	**le gâteau** lə gätō
candy	**les chocolats** m/pl lā shôkôlä
canned goods	**les conserves** f/pl lā kôNserv
carrot	**la carotte** lä kärôt
celery	**le céleri** lə sālrē
cheese	**le fromage** lə frômäzh
cherries	**les cerises** f/pl lā sərēz
chestnuts	**les marrons** m/pl lā märôN
chicken	**le poulet** lə pōōle
chocolate	**le chocolat** lə shôkôlä
chop (meat)	**la côtelette** lä kôtlet
cider	**le cidre** lə sēd'rə
cocoa	**le cacao** lə käkä-ō
coffee	**le café** lə käfā
cold cuts	**la charcuterie** lä shärkētrē
condensed milk	**le lait condensé** lə le kôNdäNsā

cookies	**les biscuits** *m/pl* lā bēskē·ē
corn	**le maïs** lə mä·ēs
cream	**la crème** lä krem
cucumber	**le concombre** lə kôNkôNb'rə
cutlet	**l'escalope** *f* leskälôp
dates	**les dattes** *f/pl* lā dät
egg	**l'œuf** *m, pl*: **les œufs** lāf, *pl*: lāzā
eggplant	**l'aubergine** *f* lōberzhēn
figs	**les figues** *f/pl* lā fēg
fish	**le poisson** lə pô·äsôN
fruit	**les fruits** *m/pl* lā frē·ē
garlic	**l'ail** *m* lä'ē
grapes	**les raisins** *m/pl* lā rezeN
ground meat	**la viande hachée** lä vyäNd äshā
ham	**le jambon** lə zhäNbôN
boiled –	**le jambon cuit** lə zhäNbôN kē·ē
smoked –	**le jambon cru** lə zhäNbôN krē
herbal tea	**l'infusion** *f* leNfēzyôN
herbs	**les fines herbes** *f/pl* lā fēnəzerb
honey	**le miel** lə myel
jam	**la confiture** lä kôNfētēr
juice	**le jus** lə zhē
ketchup	**le ketchup** lə ketshäp
lamb	**l'agneau** *m* länyō
lemon	**le citron** lə sētrôN
lettuce	**la laitue** lä letē
liver pâté	**le pâté de foie** lə pätā də fô·ä

144

margarine	**la margarine** lä märgärēn
mayonnaise	**la mayonnaise** lä mäyônez
meat	**la viande** lä vyäNd
melon	**le melon** lə melôN
milk	**le lait** lə le
skim –	**le lait demi-écrémé** lə le dəmē-äkrämä
whole –	**le lait entier** lə le äNtyā
mineral water	**l'eau** *f* **minérale** lō mēnäräl
oatmeal	**les flocons** *m/pl* **d'avoine** lā flôkôN dävô-än
oil	**l'huile** *f* lē̲-ēl
olive –	**l'huile** *f* **d'olive** lē̲-ēl dôlēv
olives	**les olives** *f/pl* lāzôlēv
onion	**l'oignon** *m* lônyôN
orange	**l'orange** *f* lôräNzh
– juice	**le jus d'orange** lə zhē̲ dôräNzh
parsley	**le persil** lə persē
pasta	**les pâtes** *f/pl* lā pät
peach	**la pêche** lä pesh
pear	**la poire** lä pô-är
pepper *(spice)*	**le poivre** lə pô-äv'rə
pepper *(vegetable)*	**le poivron** lə pô-ävrôN
pickle	**le cornichon** lə kôrnēshôN
pistacchios	**les pistaches** *f/pl* lā pēstäsh
pork	**le cochon, le porc** lə kôshôN, lə pôr
potatoes	**les pommes** *f/pl* **de terre** lā pôm də ter
poultry	**la volaille** lä vôlä'ē

6

145

pumpernickel	**le pain noir** lə peN nô·är
rice	**le riz** lə rē
rolls	**les petits pains** *m/pl* lā pətē peN
salt	**le sel** lə sel
sausage *(smoked)*	**le saucisson** lə sôsēsôN
sausage *(raw)*	**la saucisse** lä sôsēs
soft drink	**la limonade** lä lēmônäd
spices	**les épices** *f/pl* lāzpēs
spinach	**les épinards** *m/pl* lāzāpēnär
steak	**le steak** lə stek
strawberries	**les fraises** *f/pl* lā frez
sugar	**le sucre** lə sēk'rə
– cubes	**le sucre en morceaux** lə sēkräN mòrsō
tea	**le thé** lə tā
– bag	**le sachet de thé** lə säshe də tā
tomato	**la tomate** lä tômät
tuna	**le thon** lə tôN
veal	**le veau** lə vô
vegetables	**les légumes** *m/pl* lā lāgēm
vinegar	**le vinaigre** lə vēneg'rə
walnuts	**les noix** *f/pl* lā nô·ä
watermelon	**la pastèque** lä pästek
wine	**le vin** lə veN
red –	**le vin rouge** lə veN rōōzh
white –	**le vin blanc** lə veN bläN
yogurt	**le yaourt** lə ē·ä·ōōr
zucchini	**les courgettes** *f/pl* lā kōōrzhet
zwieback	**les biscottes** *f/pl* lā bēskôt

INFO Next to cheese and wine, people also associate France with the **baguette**: this long, crusty loaf of white bread is never missing from the table at any meal. There are also many other kinds of bread made from the same dough in every size and shape imaginable: for example the long, thin version of the baguette, called a **flûte** or **ficelle**, or the broad, large **pain**. Recently the French have been expanding their repertoire of bread, making for example **pain complet** (whole-wheat bread), **pain de campagne** (rustic bread), or **pain de seigle** (rye bread). You can even find the traditional white pan loaf (**pain de mie**) and crisp bread (**pain croustillant**) almost everywhere.

The **marché** (farmer's market) is held once a week; particularly if you are in southern France, you should try to visit it. The large selection of fruit and vegetables creates a colorful feast for the eyes, and you can purchase many regional specialities at good prices. The **Halles** (Parisian market halls) no longer exist, but many parts of Paris and other cities still maintain their tradition. Their covered markets are open every day, even Sunday mornings. The atmosphere in these markets is unique, well worth a visit.

SOUVENIRS

What products are typical of this area?	**Quels sont les produits régionaux typiques?** kel sôN lä prôdē·ē räzhē·ônō tēpēk?
Is this handmade?	**Est-ce que c'est fait à la main?** eskə se fe ä lä meN?
Is this *antique/genuine*?	**Est-ce que c'est *ancien/du vrai*?** eskə se äNsyeN/dē vre?

Souvenirs

belt	**la ceinture** lä seNtēr
blanket	**la couverture** lä kōōvertēr
bowl *(for drinking)*	**le bol** lə bôl
crafts	**l'artisanat** *m* lärtēzänä
dishes	**la vaisselle** lä vesel
fines herbes	**les herbes** *f/pl* **de Provence** läzerb də prôväNs
goblet	**le gobelet** lə gôble
handbag	**le sac à main** lə säk ä meN
handcrafted	**artisanal** ärtēzänäl
handcrafted item	**le produit artisanal** lə prôdē·ē ärtēzänäl
handmade	**fait à la main** fetä lä meN
jewelry	**les bijoux** *m/pl* lä bēzhōō
lace	**la dentelle** lä däNtel
lavender	**la lavande** lä läväNd
leather	**le cuir** lə kē·ēr
pottery	**la poterie** lä pôtrē

148

ceramics	**la céramique** lä särämēk
shoulder bag	**le sac à bandoulière**
	lə säk ä bäNdŌŌlyer
silk scarf	**le foulard de soie** lə fŌŌlär də sô·ä
souvenir	**le souvenir** lə sŌŌvnēr
stoneware	**la faïence** lä fäyäNs
tablecloth	**la nappe** lä näp
embroidered –	**la nappe brodée** lä näp brôdā
typical	**typique** tēpēk
vase	**le vase** lə väz

CLOTHES AND DRY CLEANER'S

I'm looking for ...   **Je cherche ...** zhə shersh ...

? **Quelle est votre taille?**   What size are you?
kel e vôt'rə tä'ē?

I'm a European size ...   **Je porte du ...** zhə pôrt dē ...

Do you have this in   **Est-ce que vous l'avez dans une autre**
another *size/color*?   *taille/couleur?* eskə vŌŌ lävā däNzēn
ôt'rə tä'ē/kŌŌlŒr?

➡ *Colors and Patterns (p. 139)*

May I try this on?   **Je peux l'essayer?** zhə pœ lāsāyā?

Do you have a mirror?   **Vous avez une glace?** vŌŌzävā ēn gläs?

What kind of material   **C'est en quel tissu?** setäN kel tisē?
is this made of?

| It doesn't fit. | **Cela ne me va pas.** |
| | səlä nə mə vä pä. |

| It's too *big/small.* | **C'est trop *grand/petit.*** |
| | se trō *gräN/pətē.* |

◆ *Basic Phrases (p. 134)*

| This fits perfectly. | **Cela va parfaitement.** |
| | səlä vä pärfetmäN. |

| I'd like to get this dry-cleaned. | **Je voudrais faire nettoyer cela.** |
| | zhə vōōdre fer netô-äyā səlä. |

| Can you get rid of this stain? | **Vous pouvez enlever cette tache?** |
| | vōō pōōvā äNləvā set täsh? |

Clothes and Dry Cleaner's

belt	**la ceinture** lä seNtēr
blouse	**le chemisier** lə shemēzyā
bra	**le soutien-gorge** lə sōōtyeN-gôrzh
cap	**le bonnet** lə bône
coat	**le manteau** lə mäNtō
collar	**le col** lə kôl
color	**la couleur** lä kōōlār
cotton	**le coton** lə kôtôN
denim	**le jean** lə dzhēn
dress	**la robe** lä rôb
to dry-clean	**nettoyer (à sec)**
	netô-äyā (ä sek)
elegant	**élégant** ālāgäN
to fit	**aller** älā

150

jacket	**la veste** lä vest
leather	**le cuir** lə kē̇·ēr
linen	**le lin** lə leN
long	**long** lôN
material	**la matière** lä mätyer
nightgown	**la chemise de nuit** lä shəmēz də nē̇·e
pants	**le pantalon** lə päNtälôN
pantyhose	**le collant** lə kôläN
scarf *(knitted)*	**l'écharpe** *f* lāshärp
scarf *(silk, silky)*	**le foulard** lə fŏŏlär
shirt	**la chemise** lä shəmēz
short	**court** kŏŏr
shorts	**le short** lə shôrt
silk	**la soie** lä sô·ä
size *(clothes)*	**la taille** lä tä′ē
size *(shoes)*	**la pointure** lä pô·eNtēr
skirt	**la jupe** lä zhēp
sleeves	**les manches** *f/pl* lā mäNsh
long –	**les manches** *f/pl* **longues** lā mäNsh lôNg
short –	**les manches** *f/pl* **courtes** lā mäNsh kŏŏrt
socks	**les chaussettes** *f/pl* lā shôset
knee –	**les mi-bas** *m/pl* lā mē-bä
sports coat	**le veston** lə vestôN
sun hat	**le chapeau de soleil** lə shäpō də sôle′ē
sweater	**le pullover** lə pēlōver

sweatsuit	**la tenue de jogging**
	lä tənē də dzhôgēng
T-shirt	**le T-shirt** lə tā-shärt
terry cloth	**le tissu éponge** lə tēsē āpôNzh
tie	**la cravate** lä krävät
to try on	**essayer** esāyā
underpants	**le slip** lə slēp
wool	**la laine** lä len

SHOES

| I'd like a pair of ... | **Je voudrais une paire de ...** |
| | zhə vōōdre ēn per də ... |

? **Quelle est votre pointure?**
kel e vôt'rə pô·eNtēr?

What size do you
take?

| I take size ... | **Ma pointure est ...** mä pô·eNtēr e ... |

| The heel is too *high/ low* for me. | **Le talon est trop *haut/plat*.** lə tälôN e trō ō/plä. |

| They're too *big/small*. | **Elles sont trop *grandes/petites*.** el sôN trō gräNd/pəfēt. |

| They're too tight around here. | **Elles me serrent ici.** el mə ser ēsē. |

Would you fix the heels, please?	**(Réparez) les talons, s'il vous plaît.**
	(rāpärā) lā tälôN, sēl vōō ple.
Could you resole the shoes, please?	**Un ressemelage, s'il vous plaît.**
	eN rəsemläzh, sēl vōō ple.

6

Shoes

boots	**les bottes** *f/pl* lā bôt
heel	**le talon** lə tälôN
hiking boots	**les chaussures** *f/pl* **de randonnée**
	lā shōsēr də räNdônā
leather	**le cuir** lə kē̄-ēr
– sole	**la semelle en cuir**
	lä səmel äN kē̄-ēr
pumps	**les escarpins** *m/pl* lāzeskärpeN
rubber boots	**les bottes** *f/pl* **en caoutchouc**
	lā bôt äN kä-ōōtshōō
rubber sole	**la semelle en caoutchouc**
	lä səmel äN kä-ōōtshōō
sandals	**les sandales** *f/pl* lā säNdäl
shoelaces	**les lacets** *m/pl* lā läse
shoes	**les chaussures** *f/pl* lā shôsēr
size	**la pointure** lä pô-eNtēr
sneakers	**les baskets** *m/pl* lā bäsket
thongs	**les sandales** *f/pl* **de bain**
	lā säNdäl də beN

WATCHES AND JEWELRY

My watch is *fast/slow*. **Ma montre *avance/retarde*.**

Could you have a look at it? **Vous pourriez la regarder?** mä môNtrə äväNs/rətärd. vōō pōōrye lä regärdä?

I'm looking for a nice *souvenir/present*. **Je cherche un joli *souvenir/cadeau*.** zhə shersh eN zhôlē *sōōvnēr/kädō*.

? **Dans quel prix?** däN kel prē?   How much would you like to pay?

What's this made of? **C'est en quoi?** setäN kô·ä?

Watches and Jewelry

battery	**la pile** lä pēl
bracelet	**le bracelet** lə bräsle
brass	**le cuivre** lə kē̲·ēv'rə
brooch	**la broche** lä brôsh
carat	**le carat** lə kärä
clip-on earrings	**les clips** *m/pl* lā klēp
costume jewelry	**le bijou fantaisie** lə bēzhōō fäNtezē
earrings	**les boucles *f/pl* d'oreille** lā bōōk'lə dôre'ē
gold	**l'or** *m* lôr
gold-plated	**doré** dôrā
necklace	**la chaîne** lä shen
pearl	**la perle** lä perl
pendant	**le pendentif** lə päNdäNtēf
plated	**plaqué** pläkā

154

ring	la bague lä bäg
silver	l'argent *m* lärzhäN
silver-plated	argenté ärzhäNtā
watch	la montre lä môNt'rə
-band	le bracelet de montre
	lə bräsle də môNt'rə

PERSONAL HYGIENE AND HOUSEHOLD

INFO The **drogueries** in France sell household goods and cleaning products, but only some personal hygiene articles such as soap or toothpaste. You can purchase cosmetics in the **parfumerie**. But recently more and more **drogueries** have started selling cosmetics.

Personal hygiene

aftershave	la lotion après rasage
	lä lôsyóN äpre räzäzh
baby bottle	le biberon lə bēbrôN
– nipple	la tétine lä tātēn
baby oil	l'huile *f* pour bébés lē̇-ēl pōōr bābā
baby powder	la poudre pour bébés
	lä pōōd(rə) pōōr bābā
bandage *(adhesive)*	le pansement adhésif
	lə päNsmäN ädāzēf
blusher	le blush lə bläsh
body lotion	la lotion corporelle lä lôsyôN kôrpôrel
brush	la brosse lä brôs

155

cleansing cream	**le lait démaquillant**
	lə le dāmäkēyäN
comb	**le peigne** lə pen'yə
condoms	**les préservatifs** *m/pl* lā präzervätēf
cotton (balls)	**le coton** lə kôtôN
cotton swabs	**les Cotons-Tiges** *m/pl (TM)*
	lā kôtôN-tēzh
dental floss	**le fil dentaire** lə fēl däNter
deodorant	**le déodorant** lə dā-ôdôräN
depilatory cream	**la crème dépilatoire**
	lā krem dāpēlätô-är
detergent	**le détergent** lə dāterzhäN
diapers	**les couches** *f/pl* lā kōōsh
disposable ...	**... à jeter** ... ä zhətā
elastic hairband	**l'élastique** *m* **à cheveux**
	lālästēk ä shəv◌̄
eye shadow	**l'ombre** *f* **à paupières**
	lôNbrə pôpyer
fragrance-free	**non parfumé** nôN pärf@mā
hair dryer	**le sèche-cheveux** lə sesh-shəv◌̄
hairspray	**la laque à cheveux** lā läk ä shəv◌̄
handcream	**la crème de soins pour mains**
	lā krem də sô-eN pōōr meN
handkerchiefs	**les mouchoirs** *m/pl* mōōshô-är
lip balm	**le stick à lèvres** lə stēk ä lev'rə
lipstick	**le rouge à lèvres** lə rōōzh ä lev'rə
mascara	**le rimmel** lə rēmel
mirror	**le miroir** lə mērô-är

mosquito repellent	**la protection anti-moustiques** lä prôteksyôN äNtē-mōōstēk
nail file	**la lime à ongles** lä lēm ä ôNg'lə
nail polish	**le vernis à ongles** lə vernē ä ôNg'lə
– remover	**le dissolvant** lə dēsôlväN
nailbrush	**la brosse à ongles** lä brôs ä ôNg'lə
night cream	**la crème de nuit** lä krem də nē̇-ē
pacifier	**la sucette** lä sẹset
perfume	**le parfum** lə pärfeN
powder	**la poudre** lä pōōd'rə
razor	**le rasoir** lə razō·är
– blade	**la lame de rasoir** lä läm də räzō·är
shampoo	**le shampooing** lə shäNpōō·eN
shaving cream	**la crème à raser** lä krem ä räzā
shaving foam	**la mousse à raser** lä mōōs ä räzä
shower gel	**le gel douche** lə zhel dōōsh
skin cream	**la crème de soins** lä krām də sô·eN
soap	**le savon** lə sävôN
SPF (sun protection factor)	**le facteur de protection solaire** lə fäktār də prôteksyôN sôler
suncream	**la crème solaire** lä krem sôler
sunscreen *(oil-based)*	**l'huile f solaire** lē̇·ēl sôler
sunscreen *(gel-based)*	**le gel solaire** lə zhel sôler
suntan lotion	**le lait solaire** lə le sôler
tampons	**les tampons** *m/pl* lā täNpôN
tissues	**les lingettes** *f/pl* lā leNzhet

157

toilet paper	**le papier hygiénique**
	lə päpyā ēzhē-ānēk
toothbrush	**la brosse à dents** lä brôs ä däN
toothpaste	**le dentifrice** lə däNtēfrēs
tweezers	**la pince à épiler** lä peNs ä āpēlā
washcloth	**le gant de toilette** lə gäN də tô·älet

Household

adapter	**l'adaptateur** *m* lädäptätār
alarm clock	**le réveil** lə rāve'ē
aluminum foil	**l'aluminium** *m* **ménager**
	lälēmēnyôm mānäzhā
barbeque	**le barbecue** lə bärbekyōō
battery	**la pile** lä pēl
bottle opener	**le décapsuleur** lə dākäpsēlār
broom	**le balai** lə bäle
bucket	**le seau** lə sō
can opener	**l'ouvre-boîte** *m* lōōv'rə-bô·ät
candle	**la bougie** lä bōōzhē
charcoal	**le charbon de bois**
	lə shärbôN də bô·ä
cleaning material	**le produit de nettoyage**
	lə prôdē·ē də netô·äyäzh
clothes pins	**les pinces** *f/pl* **à linge**
	lā peNs ä leNzh
corkscrew	**le tire-bouchon** lə tēr-bōōshôN
cup	**la tasse** lä täs

detergent	**le détergent** lə dāterzhäN
dish-washing –	**le liquide vaisselle** lə lēkēd vesel
dish cloth	**le chiffon vaisselle** lə shēfôN vesel
extension cord	**la rallonge** lä rälôNzh
flashlight	**la lampe de poche** lä läNp də pôsh
fork	**la fourchette** lä fōōrshet
gas canister	**la cartouche à gaz** lä kärtōōsh ä gäz
glass	**le verre** lə ver
insect repellent	**le spray anti-insectes** lə spre äNtē-eNsekt
knife	**le couteau** lə kōōtō
light bulb	**l'ampoule** *f* läNpōōl
lighter	**le briquet** lə brēkā
matches	**les allumettes** *f/pl* läzälēmet
methylated spirit	**l'alcool** *m* **à brûler** lälkôl ä brēlā
napkin	**la serviette** lä servyet
pan	**la poêle** lä pô·äl
paper cup	**le gobelet en carton** lə gôble äN kärtôN
paper plate	**l'assiette** *f* **en carton** läsyet äN kärtôN
plastic cutlery	**les couverts** *m/pl* **en plastique** lā kōōver äN plästēk
plastic wrap	**le film fraîcheur en polyéthylène** lə fēlm freshār äN pôlē·ätēlen
plate	**l'assiette** *f* läsyet
pocketknife	**le couteau de poche** lə kōōtō də pôsh

6

pot	**la casserole** lä käsrôl
rag *(for cleaning)*	**la serpillière** lä serpēyer
safety pin	**l'épingle** *f* **de sûreté**
	lāpeNg'lə də sẽrtā
scissors	**les ciseaux** *m/pl* lā sēzō
scrubbing brush	**le balai-brosse** lə bȧle-brôs
sewing needle	**l'aiguille** *f* **à coudre**
	legē'ē ä kōōd'rə
sewing thread	**le fil à coudre** lə fēl ä kōōd'rə
solid fire lighter	**l'allume-feu** *m* lȧlĕm-fₑ
spoon	**la cuillère** lä kē-ēyer
string	**la ficelle** lä fēsel
toothpick	**le cure-dents** lə kẽr-däN
washing line	**la corde à linge** lä kôrd ä leNzh

AT THE OPTICIAN'S

My glasses are broken.	**Mes lunettes sont cassées.**
	mā lĕnet sôN käsā.
Can you fix this?	**Pouvez-vous réparer cela?**
	pōōvā-vōō rāpärā səlä?
I'm *nearsighted/*	**Je suis** *myope/hypermétrope.*
farsighted.	zhə svē mē·ôp/ēpermätrôp.
I'd like a pair of	**Je voudrais des lunettes de soleil (avec**
(prescription) sun-	**verres correcteurs).** zhə vōōdrə dā
glasses.	lĕnet də sôle'ē (ȧvek ver kôrektₐr).

160

I've *lost/broken* a contact lens.	**J'ai *perdu/cassé* une lentille de contact.** zhā *perdĕ/käsā* ĕn läNtē'ē də kôNtäkt.	

I need some *rinsing/cleaning* solution for *hard/soft* contact lenses.	**Il me faudrait une solution de *conservation/nettoyage* pour lentilles *dures/souples*.** ĕl mə fôdre ĕn sôlĕsyôN de kôNservâsyôN/netŏ-âyäzh pōōr läNtē'ē dĕr/sōōp'lə.	

AT THE HAIRDRESSER'S

I'd like to make an appointment for ...	**Je voudrais un rendez-vous pour ...** zhə vōōdre eN räNdā-vōō pōōr ...	
? Qu'est-ce qu'on vous fait? keskôN vōō fe?		What would you like to have done?
Just a trim, please.	**Une coupe seulement.** ĕn kōōp sĕlmäN.	
I'd like my hair washed, cut, and blow-dried, please.	**Une coupe shampooing-brushing, s'il vous plaît.** ĕn kōōp shäNpōō-eN-bräshēng, sēl vōō ple.	
? Que désirez-vous comme coupe? ke dāzērā-vōō kôm kōōp?		How do you want it cut?

I'd like ...	**Je voudrais ...** zhə vōōdre ...
a perm.	**une permanente.** ēn permänäNt.
some highlights put in.	**les mèches.** lā mesh.
to have it colored.	**une coloration.** ēn kôlôräsyôN.

| Don't take too much off, please. | **Pas trop court, s'il vous plaît.** pä trō kōōr, sēl vōō ple. |

| A little more off, please. | **Un peu plus court, s'il vous plaît.** eN pä plē kōōr, sēl vōō ple. |

| Could you make ... a bit shorter, please? | **Raccourcissez un peu ..., s'il vous plaît.** räkōōrsēsä eN pä ..., sēl vōō ple. |

the back	**derrière** deryer
the front	**devant** dəväN
the sides	**de côté** də kôtā
the top	**en haut** äNō

| Part it on the *left/right*, please. | **La raie à *gauche/droite*, s'il vous plaît.** lä re ä *gôsh/drô·ät*, sēl vōō ple. |

| Please trim my beard. | **La barbe, s'il vous plaît.** lä bärb, sēl vōō ple. |

| Please give me a shave. | **Un rasage, s'il vous plaît.** eN räzäzh, sēl vōō ple. |

bangs	**la frange** lä fräNzh
beard	**la barbe** lä bärb
black	**noir** nô·är
blond	**blond** blôN
to blow-dry	**faire un brushing** fer eN bräshēng
brown	**brun** breN
to cut	**couper** kōōpā
dandruff	**les pellicules** *f/pl* lā pelēkēl
to dye	**faire une teinture** fer ēn teNtēr
gel	**le gel** lə zhel
gray	**gris** grē
hair	**les cheveux** *m/pl* lā shəvā
– coloring	**la coloration** lä kôlôräsyôN
– spray	**la laque à cheveux** lä läk ä shəvā
dry –	**les cheveux** *m/pl* **secs** lä shəvā sek
oily –	**les cheveux** *m/pl* **gras** lä shəvā grä
mustache	**la moustache** lä mōōstäsh
perm	**la permanente** lä permänäNt
razor cut	**la coupe au rasoir** lä kōōp ō räzô·är
to shave	**raser** räzā
to wash	**faire un shampooing** fer eN shäNpōō·eN

PHOTO AND VIDEO

I'd like ... **Je voudrais ...** zhə vōōdre ...

a memory card. **une carte memoire.** ēn kärt māmô·är.

a roll of film for this camera. **une pellicule pour cet appareil.** ēn pelēkēl pōōr set äpäre'ē.

a *color/black-and-white* film. **une pellicule en *couleurs/noir et blanc.*** ēn pelēkēl äN kōōlār/nô·är ā bläN.

a slide film. **une pellicule pour diapositives.** ēn pelēkēl pōōr dyäpōzētēv.

a film with *24/36* exposures. **une pellicule pour *vingt-quatre/trente-six* photos.** ēn pelēkēl pōōr veNkät'rə/träNtsēs fōtō.

I'd like some batteries for this camera. **Je voudrais des piles pour cet appareil.** zhə vōōdre dā pēl pōōr setäpäre'ē.

Could you please put the film in for me? **Vous pouvez me placer la pellicule dans l'appareil?** vōō pōōvā mə pläsā lä pelēkēl däN läpäre'ē?

Just develop the negatives, please. **Seulement les négatifs, s'il vous plaît.** sälmäN lā nāgätēf, sēl vōō ple.

I'd like a ... × ... picture from each negative, please. **Une épreuve de chaque négatif, format ... sur ..., s'il vous plaît.** ēn āprāv də shäk nāgätēf, fôrmä ... sēr ..., sēl vōō ple.

164

When will the pictures be ready?	**Les photos seront prêtes quand?** lā fōtō sərôN pret käN?
Could you repair my camera?	**Vous pouvez réparer mon appareil photo?** vōō pōōvā rāpārā mônäpäre'ē fōtō?
The film doesn't wind forward.	**Il bloque.** ēl blôk.
The *shutter release/ flash* doesn't work.	**Le déclencheur/Le flash ne fonctionne pas.** lə dākläNshạr/lə fläsh nə fôNksyôn pä.
I'd like to have passport photos taken.	**Je voudrais faire faire des photos d'identité.** zhə vōōdre fer fer dā fōtō dēdäNtētā.
Do you have any ... by ...?	**Avez-vous des ... de ...?** ävā-vōō dā ... də ...?
CD's	**CD** sā-dā
cassettes	**cassettes** käset
records	**disques** dēsk
Do you have ... 's latest cassette?	**Je voudrais la dernière cassette de ...** zhə vōōdre lä dernyer käset də ...
I'm interested in folk music. What would you recommend?	**Je m'intéresse à la musique folklorique. Pourriez-vous me recommander quelque chose?** zhə meNtāres ä lä mēzēk fôlklôrēk. pōōryā-vōō mə rəkômäNdā kelkə shōz?

automatic shutter release	**le déclencheur automatique** lə dāklāNshār ôtômätēk
battery	**la pile** lä pēl
black-and-white film	**la pellicule en noir et blanc** lä pelēkēl äN nô·är ā bläN
camcorder	**le caméscope** lə kämāskôp
camera	**l'appareil *m* photo** läpäre'ē fōtō
cassette	**la cassette** lä käset
CDs	**les CD *m/pl*** lā sā-dā
color film	**la pellicule en couleurs** lä pelēkēl äN koolär
color filter	**le filtre coloré** lə fēlt'rə kôlôrā
digital camera	**l'appareil photo numérique** läpäre'e fōtō nēmerēk
to expose	**exposer** ekspôzā
film *(camera)*	**la pellicule** lä pelēkēl
film *(movie camera)*	**le film** lə fēlm
to film	**filmer** fēlmā
flash	**le flash** lə fläsh
folk music	**la musique folklorique** lä mēzēk fôlklôrēk
lens	**l'objectif *m*** lôbzhektēv
light meter	**le posemètre** lə pōzmet'rə
light sensitivity	**la sensibilité** lä säNsēbēlētā
music	**la musique** lä mēzēk
negative	**le négatif** lə nāgätēf
photo	**la photo** lä fōtō
radio	**la radio** lä rädyō

record	**le disque** lə dēsk
shutter release	**le déclencheur** lə dākläNshār
slide	**la diapo** lä dyäpō
– film	**la pellicule pour diapositives** lä pelēkēl pōōr dyäpōzētēv
UV filter	**le filtre UV** lə fēlt'rə ē-vä
VHS	**VHS** vā-äsh-es
video camera	**la caméra vidéo** lä kämärä vēdā-ō
video cassette	**la vidéocassette** lä vēdā-ōkäset
Walkman®	**le Walkman®** lə ōō-ôkmän
wide-angle lens	**l'objectif grand angle** lôbzhektēf gräNdäNg'lə
zoom lens	**le téléobjectif, le zoom** lə tālā-ôbzhektēf, lə zōōm

6

READING AND WRITING

I'd like ...	**Je voudrais ...** zhə vōōdre ...
an *American/English* newspaper.	**un journal *américain/anglais*.** eN zhōōrnäl *ämärēkeN/äNgle*.
an *American/English* magazine.	**un magazine *américain/anglais*.** eN mägäzēn *ämärēkeN/äNgle*.
a map of the area.	**une carte de la région.** ēn kärt də lä räzhē-ôN.
Do you have a more current issue?	**Vous auriez aussi un journal plus récent?** vōōzôryā ôsē eN zhōōrnäl plē räsäN?

Do you have any books in English?	**Est-ce que vous avez des livres en anglais?** eskə vōōzävā dā lēvränäNgle?
Do you have stamps?	**Est-ce que vous avez aussi des timbres?** eskə vōōzävā ôsē dā teNb'rə?

Reading and Writing

adhesive tape	**le ruban adhésif** lə rēbäN ädäzēf
airmail paper	**le papier à lettres pour courrier aérien** lə päpyä ä let'rə pōōr kōōryä ä·äryeN
ballpoint pen	**le crayon bille** lə kreyôN bē'ē
book	**le livre** lə lēv'rə
colored pencils	**les crayons de couleur** lā kreyôN də kōōlär
coloring book	**le livre à colorier** lə lēv'rə ä kôlôryā
cookbook	**le livre de cuisine** lə lēv'rə də kē̄·ēzēn
dictionary	**le dictionnaire** lə dēksyôner
envelope	**l'enveloppe** *f* läNvəlôp
eraser	**la gomme** lä gôm
glue	**la colle** lä kôl
hiking trail map	**la carte de randonnées pédestres** lä kärt də räNdônā pädest'rə
magazine	**le magazine** lə mägäzēn
map of bicycle routes	**la carte de randonnées cyclistes** lä kärt də rändônā sēklēst
newspaper	**le journal** lə zhōōrnäl
paper	**le papier** lə päpyä

pencil	**le crayon** lə kreyôN
– sharpener	**le taille-crayon** lə tä'ē-kreyôN
picture book	**le livre d'images** lə lēv'rə dēmäzh
playing cards	**les cartes** *f/pl* **à jouer** lā kärt ä zhōō·ā
postcard	**la carte postale** lä kärt pôstäl
road map	**la carte routière** lä kärt rōōtyer
stamp	**le timbre** lə teNb'rə
stationery	**le papier á lettres** lə päpyā ä let'rə
street map	**le plan de la ville** lə pläN də lä vēl
travel guide	**le guide de voyage** lə gēd də vô·äyäzh
wrapping paper	**le papier cadeau** lə päpyā kädō
writing pad	**le carnet** lə kärne

6

AT THE TOBACCONIST'S

A pack of *filtered/unfiltered* cigarettes, please.	**Un paquet de cigarettes** *avec/sans* **filtres, s'il vous plaît.** eN päke də sēgäret ävek/säN fēlt'rə, sēl vōō ple.
A *carton/pack* of ..., please.	*Une cartouche/Un paquet* **de ..., s'il vous plaît.** ēn kärtōōsh/eN päke də ..., sēl vōō ple.
A pack of *pipe/cigarette* tobacco, please.	**Un paquet de tabac** *pour la pipe/à cigarettes,* **s'il vous plaît.** eN päke də täbä pōōr lä pēp/ä sēgäret, sēl vōō ple.
Could I have *a box of matches/a lighter*, please?	*Une boîte d'allumettes/Un briquet,* **s'il vous plaît.** ēn bô·ät däl**ə**met/eN brēke, sēl vōō ple.

169

box	**la boîte** lä bô·ät
carton	**la cartouche** lä kärtōōsh
cigarettes	**les cigarettes** *f/pl* lā sēgäret
cigarillos	**les cigarillos** *m/pl* lā sēgärēyō
cigars	**les cigares** *m/pl* lā sēgär
lighter	**le briquet** lə brēke
matches	**les allumettes** *f/pl* läzälēmet
pack	**le paquet** lə päke
pipe	**la pipe** lä pēp
– cleaner	**le cure-pipe** lə kēr-pēp
– tobacco	**le tabac pour la pipe** lə täbä pōōr lä pēp

Entertainment and Sports

SWIMMING AND WATER SPORTS

At the Beach

Is there a beach nearby?	**Est-ce qu'il y a une plage près d'ici?** eskēlyä ēn pläzh pre dēsē?
How do you get to the beach?	**Comment va-t-on à la plage?** kômäN vätôN ä lä pläzh?
Is there any shade there?	**Est-ce qu'il y a de l'ombre là-bas?** eskēlyä də lômb'rə lä-bä?
How *deep/warm* is the water?	**Quelle est la *profondeur/température* de l'eau?** kel e lä *prôfôNdär/täNpārätēr* də lō?

INFO You will see the green flag flying during good weather: it indicates that it is safe to swim within the marked area. If the yellow flag is flying, then only good swimmers should venture into the water. When the red flag is up, bathing is prohibited. In many places in France it is not at all unusual for people to be bathing topless. This is quite normal and not an occasion for you to notify the police. For those who wish to bare all, there are also separate nudist beaches. Dogs are not permitted on French beaches.

Are there strong currents here?	**Est-ce qu'il y a des courants?** eskēlyä dā kōōräN?
Is it dangerous for children?	**C'est dangereux pour les enfants?** se däNzhrä pōōr läzänfäN?

When is *low/high* tide?	**Quelle est l'heure de la marée *basse/ haute*?** kel e lär də lä märä *bäs/ōt*?
Are there jellyfish around here?	**Est-ce qu'il y a des méduses ici?** eskēlyä dā mādēz ēsē?
Where can I rent ...?	**Où est-ce qu'on peut louer ...?** ōō eskôN pā lōō·ā ...?
I'd like to rent a *lounge chair/beach umbrella*.	**Je voudrais louer *une chaise longue/ un parasol*.** zhə vōōdre lōō·ā *ēn shez lôNg/eN* päräsôl.
I'd like to go water-skiing.	**Je voudrais faire du ski nautique.** zhə vōōdre fer dē skē nōtēk.
I'd like to take *diving/ windsurfing* lessons.	**Je voudrais suivre un cours de *plon-gée/planche à voile*.** zhə vōōdre svēv'rə eN kōōr də *plôNzhā/pläNsh ä vô·äl*.
I'd like to go deep-sea fishing.	**Je voudrais aller pêcher en haute mer.** zhə vōōdre älā päshā äN ōt mer.
How much would *an hour/a day* cost?	**Quel est le tarif pour *une heure/une journée*?** kel e lə tärēf pōōr *ēnār/ēn* zhōōrnā?
Would you keep an eye on my things for a moment, please?	**Vous pourriez surveiller mes affaires un instant, s'il vous plaît?** vōō pōōryā sērvāyā mäzäfer eNeNstäN, sēl vōō ple?

7

173

| How much does it cost to get in? | **Combien coûte l'entrée?** kôNbyeN kōōt läNträ? |

| What kind of change do I need for the *lockers/hair-dryers*? | **Pour le *vestiaire/sèche-cheveux*, qu'est-ce qu'il me faut comme pièces?** pōōr lə *vestyer/sesh-shəvā̱*, keskēl mə fō kôm pyes? |

| Is there also a sauna here? | **Est-ce qu'il y a aussi un sauna?** eskēlyä ôsē eN sōnä? |

| Do I have to wear a bathing cap? | **Je dois porter un bonnet de bain?** zhə dô·ä pôrtā eN bône də beN? |

| I'd like to rent ... | **Je voudrais louer ...** zhə vōōdrē lōō·ä ... |

| a bathing cap. | **un bonnet de bain.** eN bône də beN. |

| a towel. | **une serviette.** ē̱n servyet. |
| some water wings. | **des manchettes gonflables.** dā mäNshet gôNfläb'lə. |

| Are there swimming courses for children? | **Est-ce qu'il y a des cours de natation pour enfants?** eskēlyä dā kōōr də nätäsyôN pōōr äNfäN? |

| Where's the *lifeguard/ first-aid station*? | **Où est le *maître-nageur/poste de secours*?** ōō e lə *met̲'rə-näzhạ̄r/pôst də səkōōr*? |

air mattress	**le matelas pneumatique** lə mätlä pnp̄mätēk
bathing suit	**le maillot (de bain)** lə mäyō (də beN)
bay	**la baie** lä be
beach	**la plage** lä pläzh
– umbrella	**le parasol** lə päräsôl
bikini	**le bikini** lə bēkēnē
boat	**le bateau** lə bätō
– rental	**la location de bateaux** lä lôkäsyôN də bätō
changing room	**la cabine** lä käbēn
current	**le courant** lə kōōräN
to dive	**plonger** plôNzhā
diving board	**le tremplin** lə träNpleN
diving mask	**le masque de plongée** lə mäsk də plôNzhā
diving platform	**le plongeoire** lə plôNzhô·är
fins	**les palmes** *f/pl* lä pälm
heated spa	**le bain thermal** lə beN termäl
inflatable boat	**le bateau pneumatique** lə bätō pnp̄mätēk
jellyfish	**la méduse** lä mādēz
lake	**le lac** lə läk
lifeguard	**le maître nageur** lə met'rə-näzhār
lifesaver	**la bouée de sauvetage** lä bōō·ā də sôvtäzh
lounge chair	**la chaise longue** lä shez lôNg
motorboat	**le bateau à moteur** lə bätō ä môtār

7

175

non-swimmer	**le non-nageur** lə nôN-näzhȳr
nudist beach	**la plage naturiste** lä pläzh nätēͅrēst
pedal boat	**le pédalo** lə pādälō
rowboat	**le bateau à rames** lə bätō ä räm
sailboat	**le bateau á voiles** lə bätō ä vô·äl
to go sailing	**faire de la voile** fer də lä vô·äl
sand	**le sable** lə säb'lə
sandy beach	**la plage de sable** lä pläzh də säb'lə
sauna	**le sauna** lə sōnä
to go scuba-diving	**plonger** plôNzhā
scuba gear	**l'équipement** *m* **de plongée** lākēpmäN də plôNzhā
sea urchin	**l'oursin** *m* lōōrseN
shade	**l'ombre** *f* lôNb'rə
shower	**la douche** lä dōōsh
snorkel	**le tube de plongée** lə tēb də plôNzhā
storm	**la tempête** lä täNpet
sunglasses	**les lunettes** *f/pl* **de soleil** lā lēnet də sôle'ē
suntan lotion	**la crème solaire** lä krem sôler
supervised beach	**la plage gardée** lä pläzh gärdā
surfboard	**la planche à voile** lä pläNsh ä vô·äl
to go surfing	**faire du surf** fer dē sₐrf
swimming trunks	**le caleçon de bain** lə kälsôN də beN
to go swimming *(as a sport)*	**nager** näzhā
to go swimming *(for pleasure)*	**se baigner** sə benyā
swimming pool	**la piscine** lä pēsēn

176

tide	**la marée** lä märā
high –	**la marée haute** lä märā ōt
low –	**la marée basse** lä märā bäs
towel	**la serviette** lä servyet
water	**l'eau** f lō
– polo	**le ballon de plage** lə bälôN də pläzh
– skiing	**le ski nautique** lə skē nōtēk
– wings	**les manchettes** f/pl **gonflables** lā mäNshet gôNfläb'lə
wave	**la vague** lä väg
wet suit	**la combinaison de plongée** lä kôNbēnezôN də plôNzhā
to go wind-surfing	**faire de la planche à voile** fer də lä pläNsh ä vô·äl

 More Sports and Games (p. 183)

MOUNTAINEERING

I'd like to *go to/ climb* ...	**Je voudrais** *aller à/monter sur le* **...** zhə vōōdre älä ä/môNtā sər le ...
Can you recommend *an easy/a moderately difficult* trail?	**Vous pourriez me recommander une promenade** *facile/de difficulté moyenne*? vōō pōōryā mə rəkômäNdā ēn prômnäd *fäsēl/də defēkēltā* mô·äyen?
About how long will it take?	**Combien de temps dure-t-elle environ?** kôNbyeN də täN dērtel äNvērôN?

177

INFO You can find hiking trails, indicated by the abbreviation **GR** (Grande Randonée) and a number, almost anywhere in France. They are well taken care of and always marked with two horizontal white and red stripes. You can spend the night in the **gîtes d'étape** along the way.

Is the trail well marked?	**Le chemin est bien balisé?** lə shəmeN e byeN bälēzā?
Is the trail secure?	**Les passages difficiles sont assurés?** lā pásázh dēfēsēl sôN äsē̠rā?
Is there anywhere we can get something to eat along the way?	**Est-ce qu'on trouve en route de quoi se restaurer?** eskôN trōōv äN rōōt də kô-ä sə restôrā?
Are there guided tours?	**Est-ce qu'il y a des tours guidés?** eskēlyä dā tōōr gēdā?
When does the next cable car go up?	**A quelle heure monte le prochain téléphérique?** ä kelär môNt lə prôsheN tālāfärēk?
When does the last cable car come down?	**A quelle heure descend le dernier téléphérique?** ä kelär dāsäN lə dernyā tālāfärēk?
Is this the right way to ...?	**Est-ce que c'est le bon chemin pour aller à ...?** eskə se lə bôN shəmeN pōōr älā ä ...?
How much further is it to ...?	**C'est encore loin jusqu'à ...?** setäNkôr lô·eN zhē̠skä ...?

| I'm afraid of heights. | **Je crains le vertige.** zhə kren lə vertēzh. |

Mountaineering

cable car	**le téléphérique** lə tālāfārēk
chair lift	**le télésiège** lə tālāsyezh
to go hiking	**faire des randonnées** fer dā räNdônā
hiking boots	**les chaussures** f/pl **de randonnée** lā shôsēr də räNdônā
hiking map	**la carte de randonnée** lä kärt də räNdônā
hiking trail	**le sentier de randonnée** lə säNtyā də räNdônā
hut	**le chalet** lə shäle
mountain	**la montagne** lä môNtän'yə
– climbing	**faire de la montagne** fer də lä môNtän'yə
– climbing boots	**les chaussures de montagne** lā shôsēr də môNtän'yə
– climbing guide	**le guide de montagne** lə gēd də môNtän'yə
ravine	**la gorge** lä gôrzh
rope	**la corde** lä kôrd
shelter	**le refuge** lə rəfēzh
trail	**le chemin, le sentier** lə shəmeN, lə säNtyā

7

179

SKIING

I'd like to rent ...

Je voudrais louer ... zhə vōōdre lōō·ā ...

cross-country skis.

des skis de fond. dā skē də fôN.

cross-country skiing boots, size ...

des chaussures de ski de fond, pointure ... dā shôsēr də skē də fôN, pô·eNtēr ...

downhill skis.

des skis de descente. dā skē də desäNt.

skiing boots, size ...

des chaussures de ski, pointure ... dā shôsēr də skē, pô·eNtēr ...

a snowboard.

un snowboard. eN snōbôrd.

ice skates, size ...

des patins à glace, pointure ... dā päteN ä gläs, pô·eNtēr ...

a sled.

une luge. ēn lēzh.

I'd like to ...

Je voudrais ... zhə vōōdre ...

enroll my child for skiing lessons.

inscrire mon enfant à l'école de ski. eNskrēr mônäNfäNt ä läkôl də skē.

take a skiing course.

m'inscrire à un cours de ski. meNskrēr ä eN kōōr də skē.

have a private instructor.

prendre des leçons particulières. präNd'rə dā lesôN pärtēkēlyer.

I'm ...

Je suis ... zhə svē ...

a beginner.

débutant. dābētäN.

an average skier.

un skieur moyen. eN skē·ēr mô·äyeN.

a good skier.

un bon skieur. eN bôN skē·ēr.

I'd like a lift pass for ...	**Je voudrais un forfait pour ...** zhə vōōdre eN fôrfe pōōr ...
one/half a day.	***une/une* demi-journée.** ēn/ēn dəmē-zhōōrnä.
two days.	**deux jours.** dẵ zhōōr.
a week.	**une semaine.** ēn səmen.

! **Il vous faut une photo d'iden-** **tité.** ēl vōō fō ēn fōtō dēdäNtētä.   You'll need a pass-port photo.

When is the half-day pass valid?	**Le forfait demi-journée est valable à partir de quelle heure?** lə fôrfe dəmē-zhōōrnä e väläb'lə ä pärtēr də kelär?
When do the lifts *start/stop* running?	**Les remontées marchent *à partir de/ jusqu'à* quelle heure?** lā rəmôNtā märsh *ä pärtēr də/zhē̲skä* kelär?
When is the last downhill run?	**La dernière cabine redescend à quelle heure?** lä dernyer käbēn rədāsäN ä kelär?
Has the cross-country skiing track been set?	**Est-ce que la piste de fond est pré-parée?** eskə lä pēst də fôN e präpärä?

avalanche warning	**le danger d'avalanche** lə däNzhä däväläNsh
binding	**la fixation** lä fēksäsyôN
children's pass	**le forfait enfants** lə fôrfe äNfäN
cross-country skiing	**le ski de fond** lə skē də fôN
cross-country track	**la piste de ski de fond** lä pēst də skē də fôN
downhill run	**la descente** lä dāsäNt
ice-skating	**le patinage sur glace** lə pätēnäzh sēr gläs
icy	**verglacé** vergläsā
lift	**la remontée** lä rəmôNtā
piste	**la piste** lä pēst
black –	**la piste noire** lä pēst nô·är
blue –	**la piste bleue** lä pēst blā
red –	**la piste rouge** lä pēst rōōzh
ski instructor	**le moniteur de ski** lə mônētār də skē
ski poles	**les bâtons** *m/pl* **de ski** lā bätôN də skē
ski wax	**le fart** lə färt
skiing	**le ski** lə skē
skiing goggles	**les lunettes** *f/pl* **de ski** lā lēnet də skē
skiing pass	**le forfait de ski** lə fôrfe də skē
snow	**la neige** lä nezh
toboggan course	**la piste de luge** lä pēst də lēzh

MORE SPORTS AND GAMES

Do you have any *playing cards/board games*?

Vous avez des *cartes à jouer/jeux de société*? vōōzävä dā kärt ä zhōō·ā/zhā də sôsyātā?

What sports do you participate in?

Quel sport pratiquez-vous? kel spôr prätēkā-vōō?

INFO **7** Boules or **pétanque** is not simply a sport, with boules champions sent to countless **boules** tournaments; **boules** also has an important social function: **boules** players and spectators meet at a specific place, usually in the shade of the tall, leafy plane trees, and the spectators comment on every throw. You can join the game even if you don't speak any French – as long as you know the rules.

I'd like to take a ... course.

Je voudrais suivre un cours de ... zhe vōōdre svēv're eN kōōr de ...

May I join in?

Je peux jouer avec vous? zhe pā zhōō·ā ävek vōō?

We'd like to rent a tennis court for (half) an hour.

Nous voudrions retenir un court de tennis pour une (demi-)heure. nōō vōōdrē·ôN retnēr eN kōōr de tenēs pōōr ēn (demē-)ār.

I'd like to rent ...

Je voudrais louer ... zhe vōōdre lōō·ā ...

183

aerobics	**l'aérobic** *m* lā-ārôbēk
athletic	**sportif** spôrtēf
badminton	**le badminton** lə bādmēntôn
bait	**l'appât** *m* läpä
ball *(big)*	**le ballon** lə bälôN
ball *(small)*	**la balle** lä bäl
basketball	**le basket** lə bäsket
beginner *(female)*	**la débutante** lä dābētäNt
beginner *(male)*	**le débutant** lə dābētäN
bicycle	**la bicyclette** lä bēsēklet
bike hike	**la randonnée cycliste** lä räNdônā sēklēst
board game	**le jeu de société** lə zhā də sôsyätā
canoe	**le canoë** lə känô-ā
(playing) cards	**les cartes** *f/pl* **à jouer** lā kärt ä zhōō-ā
card game	**le jeu de cartes** lə zhā də kärt
championship	**le championnat** lə shäNpyônä
changing rooms	**les vestiaires** *m/pl* lā vestyer
coach	**l'entraîneur** *m* läNtrenār
coaching session	**l'heure** *f* **d'entraîneur** lār däNtrenär
contest	**la compétition** lä kôNpātēsyôN
course	**le cours** lə kōōr
to cycle	**faire de la bicyclette** fer də lä bēsēklet
doubles *(tennis)*	**le double** lə dōōb'lə
final score	**le score** lə skôr
finishing line	**le but** lə bē
to fish	**pêcher à la ligne** peshā ä lä lēn'yə

fishing hook	**l'hameçon** *m* lämsôN
fishing license	**le permis de pêche** lə permē də pesh
fishing rod	**la canne à pêche** lä kän ä pesh
fitness center	**le studio de mise en forme**
	lə stēdyō də mēz äN fôrm
game	**la partie** lä pärtē
gliding	**le deltaplane** lə deltäplän
goal	**le but** lə bē
-keeper	**le gardien de but**
	lə gärdyeN də bē
golf	**le golf** lə gôlf
– club	**le club de golf** lə klb də gôlf
– course	**le terrain de golf** lə tereN də gôlf
gymnastics	**la gymnastique** lä zhēmnästēk
handball	**le handball** lə äNdbäl
horse	**le cheval** lə shəväl
jazz dancing	**le jazz-dance** lə dzhäz-däNs
to go jogging	**faire du jogging** fer dē dzhôgēng
judo	**le judo** lə zhēdō
kayak	**le kayak** lə käyäk
to lose	**perdre** perd'rə
mini-golf course	**le mini-golf** lə mēnē-gôlf
paragliding	**le parapente** lə päräpäNt
to play	**jouer** zhōō-ā
referee	**l'arbitre** *m* lärbēt'rə
regatta	**la régate** lä rāgät
to ride a horse	**faire du cheval** fer dē shəväl
to row	**ramer** rämā
rowboat	**le bâteau à rames** lə bätō ä räm

7

sauna	**le sauna** lə sōnä
singles *(tennis)*	**le simple** lə seNp'lə
soccer	**le football** lə fōōtbōl
– game	**le match de football** lə mätsh də fōōtbōl
– field	**le terrain de football** lə tereN də fōōtbōl
solarium	**le solarium** lə sôläryôm
sports	**le sport** lə spôr
– field	**le terrain de sport** lə tereN də spôr
squash	**le squash** lə skväsh
start	**le départ** lə däpär
table tennis	**le ping-pong** lə pēng-pôNg
team	**l'équipe** *f* lākēp
tennis	**le tennis** lə tenēs
– ball	**la balle de tennis** lä bäl də tenēs
– court	**le court de tennis** lä kōōr də tenēs
– racket	**la raquette de tennis** lä räket də tenēs
tie *(of games)*	**match nul** mätsh nēl
victory	**la victoire** lä vēktô-är
volleyball	**le volley** lə vôle
to win	**gagner** gänyā
working out *(exercise)*	**la mise en forme** lä mēz äN fôrm

186

CULTURE AND FESTIVALS

At the Box Office

à droite ä drô-ät	right	
à gauche ä gōsh	left	
complet kôNple	sold out	
la galerie lä gälrē	gallery	
la loge lä lōzh	box	
la place lä pläs	seat	
la sortie lä sôrtē	exit	
la sortie de secours lä sôrtē də səkōōr	emergency exit	
le balcon lə bälkôN	balcony	
l'entrée f läNtrā	entrance	
le milieu lə mēlyā	middle	
le parterre lə pärter	orchestra (seating)	
le rang lə räN	row	
l'orchestre m lôrkest'ər	orchestra	

Do you have a schedule of events?	**Est-ce que vous avez un calendrier des manifestations?** eskə vōōzävā eN käläNdrē-ā dā mänēfestäsyôN?

INFO French festivals often feature a **corso** (procession) or **corso fleuri** (procession of flowers). On July 14, Bastille Day, there is a **revue** (parade), **feu d'artifice** (fireworks), and a **bal du 14 juillet** (ball for the 14th of July). You might also like to visit a **fête foraine** (carnival). If you are in France during July, you might also come across the **Tour de France**, a cycling race through the entire country.

What's on today?	**Qu'est-ce qu'on donne aujourd'hui?** keskôN dôn ōzhōōrdvē?
Where can I get tickets?	**Où est-ce qu'on prend les billets?** ōō eskôN präN lā bēye?
When does the *performance/concert* start?	**A quelle heure commence *la représentation/le concert*?** ä kelār kômäNs lä rəprāzäNtäsyôN/lə kôNser?
Can I reserve tickets?	**On peut réserver?** ôN pə rāzervā?
Do you still have tickets for *today/tomorrow*?	**Vous avez encore des billets pour *aujourd'hui/demain*?** vōōzävā äNkôr dā bēye pōōr ōzhōōrdvē/dəmeN?
I'd like *a ticket/two tickets* for ..., please.	***Un billet/Deux billets* pour ..., s'il vous plaît.** eN bēye/dā bēye pōōr ..., sēl vōō ple.
How much is a ticket?	**Quel est le prix des billets?** kel e lə prē dā bēye?
Is there a discount for ...	**Est-ce qu'il y a des réductions pour ...** eskēlyä dā rādēksyôN pōōr ...
children?	**les enfants?** lāzäNfäN?
senior citizens?	**les personnes du troisième âge?** lā persôn dē trô-äsyem äzh?
students?	**les étudiants?** lāzätēdyäN?
I'd like to rent an opera glass.	**Je voudrais louer des jumelles.** zhə vōōdre lōō-ā dā zhēmel.

act	**l'acte** *m* läkt
actor	**l'acteur** *m* läktär
actress	**l'actrice** *f* läktrēs
advance booking	**la location** lä lōkäsyôN
ballet	**le ballet** lə bäle
beginning	**le début** lə dābē
box office	**la caisse** lä kes
circus	**le cirque** lə sērk
cloakroom	**le vestiaire** lə vestyer
composer	**le compositeur** lə kôNpôzētär
concert	**le concert** lə kôNser
conductor	**le chef d'orchestre** lə shef dôrkest'rə
dancer *(male)*	**le danseur** lə däNsär
dancer *(female)*	**la danseuse** lä däNsäz
director *(film)*	**le réalisateur** lə rā·älēzätär
director *(female)*	**la réalisatrice** lä rā·älēzätrēs
director *(theater)*	**le metteur en scène** lə metär äN sen
end	**la fin** lä feN
festival	**le festival** lə festēväl
folklore evening	**la soirée folklorique** lä sô·ärā fôlklôrēk
intermission	**l'entracte** *m* läNträkt
leading role	**le premier rôle** lə prəmyā rōl
movie	**le film** lə fēlm
– theater	**le cinéma** lə sēnämä
music	**la musique** lä mēsēk
musical	**la comédie musicale** lä kômādē mēzēkäl

7

189

opera	**l'opéra** *m* lôpārä
opera singer *(female)*	**la cantatrice** lä käNtätrēs
orchestra	**l'orchestre** *m* lôrkest're
original version	**la version originale** lä versyôN ôrēzhēnäl
performance *(movie)*	**la séance** lä sä·äNs
performance *(theater)*	**la représentation** lä reprāzäNtäsyôN
play	**la pièce de théâtre** lä pyes de tā·ät're
premiere	**la première** lä premyär
production	**la mise en scène** lä mēz äN sen
program	**le programme** le prôgräm
seat	**la place** lä pläs
singer *(female)*	**la chanteuse** lä shäNtēz
singer *(male)*	**le chanteur** le shäNtēr
soloist *(female)*	**la soliste** lä sôlēst
soloist *(male)*	**le soliste** le sôlēst
subtitled	**sous-titré** sōō-tētrā
subtitles	**les sous-titres** *m/pl* lā sōō-tēt're
theater	**le théâtre** le tā·ät're
ticket	**le billet d'entrée** le bēye däNtrā
vaudeville show	**les variétés** *f/pl* lä väryätā

➡️ *More Sports and Games (p. 183)*

GOING OUT IN THE EVENING

Is there a nice *bar/bistro* around here?	**Est-ce qu'il y a un bistrot sympathique par ici?** eskēlyä eN bēstrō seNpätēk pär ēsē?
Where can you go dancing around here?	**Où est-ce qu'on peut aller danser par ici?** ōō eskôN pä älä däNsä pär ēsē?
May I sit here?	**Cette place est encore libre?** set pläs etäNkôr lēb'rə?
Can you get something to eat here?	**Est-ce qu'on peut manger quelque chose ici?** eskôN pä mäNzhā kelkə shōz ēsē?

➡ *Waiter!* (p. 103)

Do you have a drinks menu?	**Est-ce que vous avez la carte des boissons?** eskə vōōzävä lä kärt dā bô·äsôN?
I'd like a *glass of wine/beer*, please.	*Un verre de vin/Une bière*, **s'il vous plaît.** eN ver də veN/ēn byer, sēl vōō ple.
The same again, please.	**La même chose, s'il vous plaît.** lä mem shōz, sēl vōō ple.
What would you like to drink?	**Qu'est-ce que *vous voulez/tu veux* boire?** keskə vōō vōōlā/tē və bô·är?

7

191

May I buy you a glass of wine?	**Est-ce que je peux *vous inviter/t'inviter* à prendre un verre de vin?** eskə zhə pä *vōōzeNvētā/teNvētā* ä präNd'rə eN ver də veN?
Would you like to dance?	**Je peux *vous inviter/t'inviter* pour cette danse?** zhə pä *vōōzeNvētā/ teNvētā* pōōr set däNs?
You dance very well.	***Vous dansez/Tu danses* très bien.** *vōō däNsā/tē däNs* tre byeN.

➡ *Small Talk (p. 19)*

Going out in the Evening

available	**libre** lēb'rə
bar	**le bar** lə bär
bistro	**le bistrot** lə bēstrō
casino	**le casino** lə käsēnō
dance	**la danse** lä däNs
to dance	**danser** däNsā
disco	**la disco, la boîte** lä dēskō, lä bô·ät
to drink	**boire** bô·är
to invite	**inviter** eNvētā
loud	**bruyant** brēyäN

ost Office, Bank, Internet

POST, TELEGRAMS, TELEPHONE

Letters and Parcels

Where is the nearest *mailbox/post office*?	**Où est la *boîte aux lettres/poste* la plus proche?** ōō e lä *bó-ät ō let′rə/pôst* lä plē prôsh?
How much does a *letter/postcard* to America cost?	**Combien coûte une *lettre/carte* aux États-Unis?** kôNbyeN kōōt ēn *let′rə/kärt* ōzātäzēnē?
Five ... stamps, please.	**Cinq timbres à ..., s'il vous plaît.** seNk teNb′rə ä ..., sēl vōō ple?
Do you have any commemorative stamps?	**Est-ce que vous avez aussi des timbres spéciaux?** eskə vōōzävā ôsē dā teNb′rə spāsyō?
I'd like a set of each, please.	**Une série de chaque, s'il vous plaît.** ēn sārē də shäk, sēl vōō ple.
I'd like to mail this *letter/package* to ..., please.	**Cette *lettre/Ce paquet* ..., s'il vous plaît.** set *let′rə/sə* päke ..., sēl vōō ple.
by airmail	**par avion** pär ävyôN
express	**par exprès** pär ekspre
by surface mail	**par voie ordinaire** pär vô-ä ôrdēner
I'd like to send a package.	**Je voudrais poster un colis.** zhə vōōdre pôstā eN kôlē.

Could you send a fax for me?	**Vous pouvez envoyer un fax pour moi?** vōō pōōvā äNvô·äyä eN fäks pōōr mô·ä?
Can I send a telegram here?	**Est-ce que je peux envoyer un télé-gramme à partir d'ici?** eskə zhə pä eNvô·äyä eN tālāgräm ä pärter dēsē?
Please give me a form for a telegram.	**Donnez-moi un formulaire de télé-gramme, s'il vous plaît.** dônā-mô·ä eN fôrmēler də tālāgräm, sēl vōō ple.
Where can I make a phone call?	**Où est-ce que je peux téléphoner ici?** ōō eskə zhə pä tālāfônä ēsē?
Could you tell me where I might find a phone booth?	**Vous pourriez m'indiquer une cabine téléphonique, s'il vous plaît?** vōō pōōryā meNdēkā ēn käbēn tālāfônēk, sēl vōō ple?

8

! **Prenez la cabine ...**   Go into booth ...
! prənā lä käbēn ...

INFO If you would like to use the public phones in France, it might be wise to buy a **télécarte** (tele-phone card), since most of the public phones in France are ope-rated with one of these. The **télécarte** is a chip card loaded with a certain amount of money; you slip it into the phone before dial-ing. You can purchase a **télécarte** in most post offices, at news-stands and **bureaux de tabac** (tobacconist's) indicated by the sign **"Ici, vente de télécartes"**.

Excuse me, could you give me change to make a phone call?	**Excusez-moi, il me faudrait des pièces pour téléphoner.** ekskēzā-mô-ä, ēl mə fôdre dā pyes pōōr tālāfônā.
Can you give me change for this bill?	**Vous pourriez me changer ce billet?** vōō pōōryā mə shäNzhā sə bēye?
What's the area code for ...?	**Quel est l'indicatif de ...?** kel e leNdēkätēf də ...?
Do you have a phone book for ...?	**Est-ce que vous avez un annuaire de ...?** eskə vōōzävā eNänē-er də ...?

INFO If you wish to phone America, dial "1" for the United States and Canada and then the area code and phone number with no further prefix.

!	**La ligne est occupée.** lä lēn'yə etôkēpā.	The line is busy.
!	**Ça ne répond pas.** sä nə rāpoN pä.	There's no answer.
!	**Essayez encore une fois.** esāyā äNkôr ēn fô-ä.	You'll have to try again.

When do evening rates apply?	**Le tarif de nuit est valable à partir de quelle heure?** lə tärēf də nē-ē e väläb'lə ä pärtēr də kelār?

address	**l'adresse** *f* lädres
addressee	**le destinataire** lə destēnäter
airmail	**par avion** pär ävyôN
area code	**l'indicatif** *m* leNdēkätēf
busy	**occupé** ôkēpā
to call (on the phone)	**téléphoner** tālāfônā
card-operated phone	**le téléphone à carte** lə tālāfôn ä kärt
C.O.D.	**contre remboursement** kôNt'rə räNbōōrsmäN
charge	**la taxe** lä täks
coin	**la pièce** lä pyes
collect call	**la communication en PCV** lä kômēnēkäsyôN äN pā-sā-vā
commemorative stamp	**le timbre spécial** lə teNb'rə spāsyäl
to connect (a call)	**passer** päsā
counter	**le guichet** lə gēshe
customs declaration	**la déclaration de douane** lä dāklärāsyôN də dōō-än
cut off	**coupé** kōōpā
declaration of value	**la valeur déclarée** lä väl̲ār dāklärā
evening rate	**le tarif de nuit** lə tärēf də nē̲-ē
express letter	**la lettre exprès** lä letrekspre
fax	**le (télé)fax** lə (tālā)fäks
international call	**la communication internationale** lä kômēnēkäsyôN eNternäsyônäl
letter	**la lettre** lä let'rə

8

197

mailbox	**la boîte aux lettres** lä bô·ät ō let'rə
package	**le colis** lə kôlē
– info form	**le bulletin d'expédition** lə bᵉlteN dekspädēsyôN
parcel	**le paquet** lə päke
pay phone	**le téléphone à pièces** lə täläfôn ä pyes
post office	**la poste** lä pôst
postcard	**la carte postale** lä kärt pôstäl
to send	**envoyer** äNvô·äyā
sender	**l'expéditeur** *m* lekspādētār
stamp	**le timbre** lə teNb'rə
– vending machine	**le distributeur automatique de timbres** lə dēstrēbᵉtār ôtômätēk də teNb'rə
telegram	**le télégramme** lə tālägräm
telephone	**le téléphone** lə tālāfôn
– booth	**la cabine téléphonique** lä käbēn tālāfônēk
– card	**la télécarte** lä tālākärt
– call	**la communication** lä kômēnēkäsyôN
– directory	**l'annuaire** *m* länē̄·er

MONEY MATTERS

Can you tell me where I can find a bank around here?	**Pardon, vous pourriez m'indiquer une banque dans le coin?** pårdôN, vōō pōōryä meNdēkä ēn bäNk däns lə kô·eN?
Where can I exchange foreign currency?	**Où est-ce que je peux changer de l'argent?** ōō eskə zhə pā shäNzhā də lärzhäN?
What's the commission charge?	**A combien s'élèvent les frais?** ä kôNbyeN sälev lā fre?
What time does the bank close?	**La banque est ouverte jusqu'à quelle heure?** lä bäNk etōōvert zhēskä kelär?

INFO Bank opening hours can vary widely. Banks are usually closed between noon and 2 p.m. And even if the bank is open, the window money-exchange might be closed. Banks are closed on Saturdays and Sundays. Some banks have countryside branches that are open only one, two, or three days a week.

8

| I'd like to change ... dollars into euros. | **Je voudrais changer ... dollars en euros.** zhə vōōdre shäNzhā ... dôlär äN ārō'. |
| Someone is wiring me some money. Has it arrived yet? | **J'attends un virement télégraphique. Est-ce que l'argent est arrivé?** zhätäN eN vērmäN tālägräfēk. eskə lärzhäN etärēva? |

199

INFO In areas frequented by tourists you can find money-exchange bureaus either at the train station or at the tourist-information office (**syndicat d'initiative, office du tourisme**). They are also located at large highway rest stops and within the city of Paris. As with the banks, they all have differing opening hours. Exchange bureaus often have exorbitant exchange rates, so it might be wise to inquire about the rate before exchanging your money.

Can I use my credit card to get cash?	**Est-ce que je peux retirer de l'argent liquide avec ma carte de crédit?** eskə zhə pā rətērā də lärzhäN lēkēd ävek mä kärt də krādē?	
I'd like to cash a traveler's check.	**Je voudrais encaisser un chèque de voyage.** zhə vōōdre äNkesā eN shek də vô-äyäzh.	
What's the highest amount I can cash?	**Quelle est la somme maximum?** kel e lä sôm mäksēmôm?	

! **Pour retirer l'argent, passez à la caisse, s'il vous plaît.** pōōr rətērā lärzhäN, päsā ä lä kes, sēl vōō ple. / You can pick up the money at the cashier.

? **Vous le voulez comment?** vōō lə vōōlā kômäN? / How would you like the money?

In small bills, please.	**Donnez-moi des petites coupures, s'il vous plaît.** dônā-mô·ä dā pətēt kōōpēr, sēl vōō ple.	

| Please give me some change, too. | **Donnez-moi aussi un peu de monnaie.** |
| | dônā-mô·à ôsē eN pā də mône. |

Money matters

amount	**le montant** lə môNtäN
ATM	**la billetterie** lä bēyetrē
bank	**la banque** lä bäNk
– account	**le compte en banque**
	lə kôNt äN bäNk
– code	**le code établissement**
	lə kôd ātäblēsmäN
– transfer	**le virement (bancaire)**
	lə vērmäN (bäNker)
bill	**le billet (de banque)**
	lə beye (də bäNk)
card number	**le numéro de la carte**
	lə nēmārô də lä kärt
cash	**l'argent** *m* **liquide** lärzhäN lēkēd
cashier	**la caisse** lä kes
change	**la monnaie** lä mône
check	**le chèque** lə shek
commission fee	**les frais** *m/pl* lā fre
counter	**le guichet** lə gēshe
credit card	**la carte de crédit** lä kärt də krādē
currency-exchange office	**le bureau de change**
	lə bērō də shäNzh
to exchange *(money)*	**changer** shäNzhā
exchange rate	**le cours** lə kōōr
money	**l'argent** *m* lärzhäN

8

receipt	**la quittance** lä kētäNs
savings account	**le livret de caisse d'épargne**
	lə lēvrе də kes dāpärn'yə
to sign	**signer** sēnyā
signature	**la signature** lä sēnyätēr
traveler's check	**le chèque de voyage**
	lə shek də vô·äyäzh
to withdraw	**retirer** rətērā

INTERNET

Where's an internet café around here?	**Où y a-t-il un cybercafé ici?** ōō yätēl eN sēberkäfe ēsē?
I'd like to send an e-mail.	**Je voudrais envoyer un courriel.** zhə vōōdrā äNvô·äyā eN kōōrēyäl.
Which computer can I use?	**Quel ordinateur est-ce que je peux utiliser?** kel ôrdēnadēr eskə zhə pē ētēlēzē?
How much is ist for 15 minutes?	**Combien coûte quinze minutes?** kôNbyeN kōōt keNz mēnēt?
Could you help me, please?	**Pourriez-vous m'aider?** pōōryā vōō mādā?

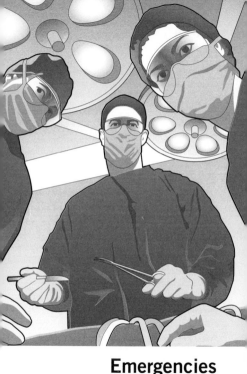

Emergencies

HEALTH

Information

Could you recommend a general practitioner?	**Est-ce que vous pouvez me recommander un médecin généraliste?** eskə vōō pōōvā mə rəkômäNdā eN mädseN zhänärälēst?
Does he speak English?	**Est-ce qu'il parle anglais?** eskēl pärl äNgle?
What are his office hours?	**Quelles sont ses heures de consultation?** kel sôN sāzər də kôNsēltäsyôN?
Can he come here?	**Est-ce qu'il pourrait venir?** eskēl pōōre vənēr?
My *husband/wife* is sick.	***Mon mari/Ma femme* est malade.** môN märē/mä fäm e mäläd.

INFO S.A.M.U. sämē is the name of the emergency assistance you can reach anytime from anywhere in France by dialling the number "15." They will arrange for emergency services and ambulances. In an emergency you can also contact **les pompiers** lā pôNpyä (the fire department).

Please call *an ambulance/the emergency service*!	**Appelez *une ambulance/le S.A.M.U.*, s'il vous plaît.** äplā ēn äNbēläNs/lə sämē, sēl vōō ple.
Where are you taking *him/her*?	**Vous *le/la* transportez où?** vōō lə/lä träNspôrtā ōō?

| I'd like to come with you. | **Je voudrais venir avec.** |
| | zhə vōōdre vənēr ävek. |

| Where's the nearest (24-hour) pharmacy? | **Où est la pharmacie (de garde) la plus proche?** ōō e lä färmäsē (də gärd) lä plē prôsh? |

Drugstore

| Do you have anything for ...? | **Vous avez quelque chose contre ...?** vōōzävä kelkə shōz kôNt'rə ...? |

| How should I take it? | **Comment est-ce que je dois le prendre?** kômäN eskə zhə dô·ä lə präNd'rə? |

| I need this medicine. | **J'ai besoin de ce médicament.** zhā bezô·eN də sə mädēkämäN. |

| **!** **Ce médicament est uniquement délivré sur ordonnance.** sə mädēkämäN etēnēkmäN dālēvrā sēr ôrdônäNs. | You need a prescription for this medicine. |

| **!** **Nous ne l'avons pas en magasin.** nōō nə lävôN pä äN mägäzeN. | I'm sorry, but we don't have that here. |

| **!** **Nous devons le commander.** nōō dəvôN lə kômäNdä. | We'll have to order it. |

| When can I pick it up? | **Vous l'aurez quand?** vōō lôrā käN? |

9

Instructions

à jeun ä zhāN	on an empty stomach
après les repas äpre lā rəpä	after meals
avaler sans croquer ävälā säN krôkā	swallow whole
avant les repas äväN lā rəpä	before meals
conformément aux prescriptions du médecin kôNfôrməmäN ō preskrēpsyôN dē mädseN	according to the doctor's instructions
contre-indications kôNtreNdēkäsyôN	contraindications
effets secondaires efe səkôNder	side effects
externe ekstern	external
interne eNtern	internal
laisser fondre dans la bouche lāsā fôNd're däN lä bōōsh	to dissolve on the tongue
rectal rektäl	rectally
trois fois par jour trô·ä fô·ä pär zhōōr	three times a day

Drugstore

antibiotic	**l'antibiotique** *m* läNtēbē·ôtēk
antiseptic ointment	**la pommade cicatrisante** lä pômäd sēkätrēzäNt
bandages	**les pansements** *m/pl* lā päNsmäN
Band-Aid®	**le pansement** lə päNsmäN
(birth-control) pill	**la pilule contraceptive** lä pēlēl kôNträseptēv
charcoal tablets	**des comprimés** *m/pl* **de charbon** dā kôNprēmā də shärbôN
condoms	**les préservatifs** *m/pl* lā präservätēf

cotton	**le coton hydrophile** lə kôtôN idrôfēl
cough syrup	**le sirop contre la toux** lə sērō kôNt'rə lä tōō
disinfectant	**le désinfectant** lə däzeNfektäN
drops	**les gouttes** *f/pl* lä gōōt
drugstore	**la pharmacie** lä färmäsē
elastic bandage	**la bande élastique** lä bäNd ālästēk
gauze bandage	**la bande de gaze** lä bäNd də gäz
homeopathic	**homéopathique** ômä·ôpätēk
injection	**la piqûre** lä pēkēr
iodine	**l'iode** *m* lyôd
laxative	**le laxatif** lə läksätēf
medicine to improve blood circulation	**le médicament pour la circulation du sang** lə mädēkämäN pōōr lä sērkäläsyôN dē säN
medicine to reduce fever	**le fébrifuge** lə fābrēfēzh
night duty	**la garde de nuit** lä gärd də nē·ē
ointment	**la pommade** lä pômäd
– for mosquito bites	**la pommade contre les piqûres de moustiques** lä pômäd kôNt'rə lä pēkēr də mōōstēk
– for sunburn	**la pommade contre les coups de soleil** lä pômäd kôNt'rə lä kōō də sôle'ē
painkiller	**l'analgésique** *m* länälzhäzēk
prescription	**l'ordonnance** *f* lôrdônäNs
sanitary napkin	**la serviette hygiénique** lä servyet ēzhē·änēk

| sleeping pills | **le somnifère** lə sômnēfer |
| something for ... | **le remède contre ...** lə rəmed kôNt'rə |

➡️ *Diseases, Doctor, Hospital (p. 217)*

suppository	**le suppositoire** lə sēpôzētô·är
tablets for ...	**les comprimés** *m/pl* **contre ...** lā kôNprēmā kôNt'rə ...
tampons	**les tampons** *m/pl* lā täNpôN
thermometer	**le thermomètre médical** lə termōmet'rə mādēkäl
tranquilizer	**le calmant** lə kälmäN

At the Doctor´s

| I have a (bad) cold. | **J'ai un (gros) rhume.** zhā eN (grō) rēm. |

| I have *diarrhea/a fever*. | **J'ai la diarrhée/fièvre.** zhā lä dyärā/fyev'rə. |

| I'm constipated. | **Je suis constipé.** zhə svē kôNstēpā. |

| My ... *hurts/hurt*. | **J'ai mal à/aux ...** zhā mäl ä/ō ... |

➡️ *Parts of the Body and Organs (p. 215)*

| I have pains here. | **J'ai mal ici.** zhā mäl ēsē. |

INFO Doctors in France are addressed simply as **"Docteur"** dôktār without **Monsieur** məsyā, **Madame** mädäm or last name. Make sure you bring your health-insurance information with you.

I've been vomiting (a lot).	**J'ai vomi (plusieurs fois).** zhā vômē (plē̲syār fô·ä).
My stomach is upset.	**J'ai un embarras d'estomac.** zhā eNäNbärä destômä.
I can't move ...	**Je ne peux pas bouger ...** zhə nə pā pä bōōzhä ...

➡ *Parts of the Body and Organs (p. 215)*

I've hurt myself.	**Je me suis blessé.** zhə mə svē blesä.
I had a fall.	**Je suis tombé.** zhə svē tôNbā.
I've been *stung/bitten* by ...	**J'ai été *piqué/mordu* par ...** zhā ātā *pēkā/môrdē̲* pär ...

9

I have (not) been vaccinated against ...	**Je (ne) suis (pas) vacciné contre ...** zhə (nə) svē (pä) väksēnä kôNt'rə ...
My last tetanus shot was about ... years ago.	**Ma dernière vaccination contre le tétanos remonte à ... ans environ.** mä dernyer väksēnäsyôN kôNt'rə lə tātänôs rəmôNt ä ... äN äNvērôN.
I'm allergic to penicillin.	**Je suis allergique à la pénicilline.** zhə svē älerzhēk ä lä pānēsēlēn.
I have high/low blood pressure.	**Je souffre d'hypertension/d'hypotension.** zhə sōōf'rə dēpertäNsyôN/ dēpôtäNsyôN.
I have a pacemaker.	**Je porte un stimulateur (cardiaque).** zhə pôrt eN stēmēlätär (kärdyäk).
I'm four months pregnant.	**Je suis enceinte de quatre mois.** zhə svē äNseNt də kät'rə mô·ä.
I'm diabetic.	**Je suis diabétique.** zhə svē dyäbātēk.
I'm HIV-positive.	**Je suis ♂ séropositif/♀ séropositive.** zhə svē ♂ sārôpôzētēf/♀ sārôpôzētēv.
I take this medicine regularly.	**Je prends régulièrement ces médicaments.** zhə präN rāgēlyermäN sā mādēkämäN.

What the Doctor says

Qu'est-ce que vous avez comme problèmes? keskə vōōzävä kôm prôblem?	What are your symptoms?
Où avez-vous mal? ōō ävā-vōō mäl?	Where does it hurt?
Ici, vous avez mal? ēsē, vōōzävä mäl?	Does this hurt?
Ouvrez la bouche. ōōvrā lä bōōsh.	Open your mouth.
Montrez la langue. môNtrā lä läNg.	Show me your tongue.
Toussez. tōōsā.	Cough.
Déshabillez-vous, s'il vous plaît. dāzäbēyā-vōō, sēl vōō ple.	Would you get undressed, please.
Relevez votre manche, s'il vous plaît. relvā vôt'rə mäNsh, sēl vōō ple.	Would you roll up your sleeve, please.
Inspirez profondément. Ne respirez plus. ēNspērā prôfôNdəmäN. nə respērā plē.	Breathe deeply. Now hold your breath.
Depuis quand avez-vous ces problèmes? dəpē̄-ē̄ käN ävä-vōō sā prôblem?	How long have you felt this way?
Est-ce que vous êtes vacciné contre ...? eskə vōōzet väksēnā kôNt'rə ...?	Have you been vaccinated against ...?

9

211

Nous devons vous faire une radio.
nōō dəvôN vōō fer ən rädyō.

We need to take some X-rays.

Vous avez une *fracture/entorse* de ...
vōōzävä ən fräktēr/äNtôrs də ...

Your ... is *broken/sprained*.

Il faut faire une analyse *de sang/d'urine*. ēl fō fer ən änälēz də säN/dēren.

We need to take a *blood/urine* sample.

Il faut vous opérer. ēl fō vōōzôpārā.

You'll have to have an operation.

Je dois vous envoyer chez un spécialiste. zhə dô·ä vōōzäNvô·äyā shā eN spāsyälēst.

I'll have to refer you to a specialist.

Ce n'est rien de grave.
se ne rē·eN də gräv.

It's nothing serious.

Vous en prendrez ... *comprimés/gouttes* ... fois par jour. vōōzäN präNdrā ... *kôNprēmā/gōōt* ... fô·ä pär zhōōr.

Take ... *tablets/drops* ... times a day.

Revenez *demain/dans* ... *jours*.
revnā *dəmeN/däN* ... *zhōōr*.

Come back *tomorrow/in* ... *days*.

Ask the Doctor

Is it serious?	**C'est grave?** se gräv?
Can you give me a doctor's certificate?	**Est-ce que vous pourriez me faire un certificat?** eskə vōō pōōryā mə fer eN sertēfēkä?
Do I have to come back again?	**Est-ce que je dois revenir?** eskə zhə dô·ä revnēr?
What precautions should I take?	**Quelles précautions dois-je prendre?** kel präkôsyôN dô·äzh präNd'rə?
Could you give me a receipt (in English) for my medical insurance?	**Pourriez-vous me donner une quittance (en anglais) pour mon assurance, s'il vous plaît?** pōōryā-vōō mə dônä ēn kētäNs (änäNgle) pōōr mônäsē̠räNs, sēl vōō ple?

In the Hospital

Is there anyone here who speaks English?	**Est-ce qu'il y a ici quelqu'un qui parle anglais?** eskēlyä ēsē kelkeN kē pärl äNgle?
I'd like to speak to a doctor.	**Je voudrais parler à un médecin.** zhə vōōdre pärlä ä eN mädseN.

➡ *At the Doctor's (p. 208)*

What's the diagnosis?	**Quel est le diagnostic?** kel e lə dyägnôstēk?

I'd rather have the operation in the U.S.	**Je préfère me faire opérer aux Etats-Unis.** zhə prāfĕr mə fer ôpārā ōzātāzēnē.
I'm insured for the journey home to the U.S.	**Mon assurance couvre les frais de rapatriement aux États-Unis.** mônäsērāNs kōōv'rə lā fre də räpätrēmāN ōzätāzēnē.
Would you please notify my family?	**Prévenez ma famille, s'il vous plaît.** prāvnā mä fämē'ē, sēl vōō ple.
Here's the *address/telephone number*.	**Voici *l'adresse/le numéro de téléphone*.** vô-äsē *lädres/lə nēmārō* də tālāfôn.
How long will I have to stay here?	**Je dois rester ici encore combien de temps?** zhə dô-ä restā ēsē äNkôr kôNbyeN də täN?
When can I get out of bed?	**Quand est-ce que je pourrai me l ever?** käNdeskə zhə pōōrā mə ləvä?
Could you give me *something for the pain/to go to sleep*?	**Donnez-moi quelque chose *contre la douleur/pour dormir*, s'il vous plaît.** dônā-mô·ä kelkə shōz *kôNt'rə lä dōōlär/pōōr dôrmēr*, sēl vōō ple.
I'd like to be discharged. (I'll assume full responsibility.)	**Je voudrais sortir de l'hôpital. (C'est à mes risques et périls.)** zhə vōōdre sôrtēr də lôpētäl. (setä mā rēsk ā pārēl.)

Parts of the Body and Organs

abdomen	**le ventre** lə väNt'rə
ankle	**la cheville** lä shəve'ē
appendix	**l'appendice** *m* läpäNdēs
arm	**le bras** lə brä
back	**le dos** lə dō
bladder	**la vessie** lä vesē
bone	**l'os** *m* lôs
chest	**la poitrine** lä pô·ätrēn
collarbone	**la clavicule** lä klävekēl
(intervertebral) disk	**le disque intervertébral** lə dēsk eNtervertābräl
ear	**l'oreille** *f* lôre'ē
-drum	**le tympan** lə teNpäN
eye	**l'œil** *m, pl:* **les yeux** lā'ē, *pl:* lāzyā
finger	**le doigt** lə dô·ä
foot	**le pied** lə pyā
forehead	**le front** lə frôN
gallbladder	**la bile** lä bēl
hand	**la main** lä meN
head	**la tête** lä tet
heart	**le cœur** lə kār
hip	**la hanche** lä äNsh
intestines	**les intestins** *m/pl* läzeNtesteN
joint	**l'articulation** *f* lärtēkēläsyôN
kidney	**le rein** lə reN
knee	**le genou** lə zhənōō
-cap	**la rotule** lä rôtēl
leg	**la jambe** lä zhäNb

9

liver	**le foie** lə fôˑä
lungs	**les poumons** *m/pl* lā pōōmôN
mouth	**la bouche** lä bōōsh
muscle	**le muscle** lə mēsk'lə
neck *(in general)*	**le cou** lə kōō
neck *(nape)*	**la nuque** lä nēk
nerve	**le nerf** lə ner
nose	**le nez** lə nā
penis	**le pénis** lə pānēs
rib	**la côte** lä kôt
shoulder	**l'épaule** *f* lāpōl
sinus	**le sinus frontal** lə sēnēs frôNtäl
skin	**la peau** lä pō
spine	**la colonne vertébrale** lä kôlôn vertābräl
stomach	**l'estomac** *m* lestōmä
temple	**la tempe** lä täNp
tendon	**le tendon** lə täNdôN
thigh	**la cuisse** lä kẹ̄ˑēs
throat	**la gorge** lä gôrzh
thyroid	**la thyroïde** lä tērôˑed
toe	**l'orteil** *m* lôrte'ē
tongue	**la langue** lä läNg
tooth	**la dent** lä däN
torso	**le haut du corps** lə ō dẹ̄ kôr
vagina	**le vagin** lə väzheN
vertebra	**la vertèbre** lä verteb'rə

AIDS	**le sida** lə sēdä
allergy	**l'allergie** *f* lälerzhē
appendicitis	**l'appendicite** *f* läpäNdēsēt
asthma	**l'asthme** *m* läsm
bite	**la morsure** lä môrsēr
bleeding	**le saignement** lə senyəmäN
blister	**l'ampoule** *f* läNpōōl
blood	**le sang** lə säN
blood poisoning	**l'empoisonnement** *m* **du sang** läNpô·äsônmäN dē säN
blood pressure	**la tension (sanguine)** lä täNsyôN (säNgēn)
high –	**l'hypertension** *f* lēpertäNsyôN
low –	**l'hypotension** *f* lēpôtäNsyôN
blood transfusion	**la transfusion de sang** lä träNsfēzyôN də säN
blood type	**le groupe sanguin** lə grōōp säNgeN
broken	**cassé** käsā
bruise	**la contusion** lä kôNtēzyôN
burn	**la brûlure** lä brēlēr
cardiac arrest	**l'infarctus** *m* leNfärktēs
(plaster) cast	**le plâtre** lə plät'rə
(doctor's) certificate	**le certificat (médical)** lə sertēfēkä (mādēkäl)
chicken pox	**la varicelle** lä värēsel
circulation problems	**les troubles** *m/pl* **circulatoires** lā trōōb'lə sērkēlätô·är

9

colic	**la colique** lä kôlēk
concussion	**la commotion cérébrale** lä kômôsyôN säräbräl
conjunctivitis	**la conjonctivite** lä kôNzhôNktēvēt
constipation	**la constipation** lä kôNstēpäsyôN
contagious	**contagieux** kôNtäzhyā
cough	**la toux** lä tōō
cramp	**la crampe** lä kräNp
cystitis	**la cystite** lä sēstēt
dermatologist	**le dermatologue** lə dermätôlôg
diabetes	**le diabète** lə dyäbet
diarrhea	**la diarrhée** lä dyärä
dislocated	**luxé** lēksä
dizziness	**les vertiges** *m/pl* lā vertēzh
doctor *(male)*	**le médecin** lə mädseN
doctor *(female)*	**la femme médecin** lä fäm mädseN
ear infection	**l'otite** *f* lôtēt
ear, nose, and throat doctor (ENT)	**l'oto-rhino-laryngologiste** *m* lôtô-rēnô-läreNgôlôzhēst
to faint	**s'évanouir** sāväNōō-ēr
fever	**la fièvre** lä fyev'rə
flu	**la grippe** lä grēp
food poisoning	**l'intoxication** *f* **alimentaire** leNtôksēkäsyôN älēmäNter
fungal infection	**la mycose** lä mēkōz
gallstones	**le calcul biliaire** lə kälkēl bēlyer
general practitioner	**le médecin généraliste** lə mädseN zhānärälēst
German measles	**la rubéole** lä rēbā·ôl

218

gynecologist *(male/female)*	*le/la* **gynécologue** lə/lä zhēnäkôlôg
hay fever	**le rhume des foins** lə rēm dā fô·eN
headache	**le mal de tête** lə mäl də tet
heart	**le cœur** lə kãr
– attack	**la crise cardiaque** lä krēz kärdyäk
– defect	**l'anomalie *f* cardiaque** länômälē kärdyäk
hernia	**la hernie** lä ernē
herpes	**l'herpès** *m* lerpes
hospital	**l'hôpital** *m* lôpētäl
infection	**l'infection** *f* leNfeksyôN
inflammation	**l'inflammation** *f* leNflämäsyôN
injury	**la blessure** lä blesēr
internist	**le spécialiste des maladies internes** lə späsyälēst dā mälädē eNtern
kidney stones	**les calculs** *m/pl* **rénaux** lä kälkēl rānô
lumbago	**le lumbago** lə lôNbägô
measles	**la rougeole** lä rōōzhôl
menstruation	**la menstruation** lä mäNstrē·äsyôN
migraine	**la migraine** lä mēgren
mumps	**les oreillons** *m/pl* läzôrāyôN
nausea	**les nausées** *f/pl* lä nōzā
nosebleed	**les saignements** *m/pl* **de nez** lä senyəmäN də nā
office hours	**les heures** *f/pl* **de consultation** läzãr də kôNsēltäsyôN

to operate on	**opérer** ôpārā
ophthalmologist	**l'oculiste** *m* lôkēlēst
orthopedist	**l'orthopédiste** *m* lôrtôpādēst
pacemaker	**le stimulateur (cardiaque)**
	lə stēmēlätār (kärdyäk)
pain(s)	**les douleurs** *f/pl* lā dōōlār
pediatrician	**le pédiatre** lə pādyät'rə
pneumonia	**la pneumonie** lä pnämônē
pregnant	**enceinte** äNseNt
to prescribe	**prescrire** preskrēr
pulled ligament	**l'élongation** lälôNgäsyôN
pulled muscle	**le claquage musculaire**
	lə kläkäzh mēskēler
pulled tendon	**l'élongation** *f* lälôNgäsyôN
pus	**le pus** lə pē
rheumatism	**les rhumatismes** lə rēmätēsm
scarlet fever	**la scarlatine** lä skärlätēn
shivering	**les frissons** *m/pl* lā frēsôN
shock	**le choc** lə shôk
sore throat	**le mal de gorge** lə mäl də gôrzh
sprained	**foulé** fōōlā
sting	**la piqûre** lä pēkēr
stomachache	**le mal d'estomac** lə mäl destômä
stroke	**l'attaque** *f* **(d'apoplexie)**
	lätäk (däpôpleksē)
sunstroke	**l'insolation** *f* leNsôläsyôN
sunburn	**le coup de soleil** lə kōō də sôle'ē
sweating	**les sueurs** *f/pl* lā sē.ār
swelling	**l'enflure** *f* läNflēr

tetanus	**le tétanos** lə tātänôs
tick	**la tique** lä tēk
torn ligament	**la déchirure** lä däshērēr
ulcer *(stomach)*	**l'ulcère** *m* **d'estomac**
	lēlser destôma
urine analysis	**l'analyse** *f* **d'urines** länälēz dērēn
urologist	**l'urologue** *m* lērôlôg
vaccination	**la vaccination** lä väksēnäsyôN
– record	**le carnet de vaccination**
	lə kärne də väksēnäsyôN
veterinarian	**le vétérinaire** lə vātärēner
vomiting	**les vomissements** *m/pl*
	lä vômēsmäN
ward	**le service** lə servēs
to X-ray	**faire une radio** fer ēn rädyō

At the Dentist's

This tooth hurts.	**J'ai mal à cette dent.**
	zhā mäl ä set däN.
This tooth is broken.	**La dent s'est cassée.** lä däN se käsā.
I've lost a filling.	**J'ai perdu un plomb.**
	zhā perdē eN plôN.
Can you do a tempo-	**Est-ce que vous pourriez soigner la**
rary job on my tooth?	**dent de façon provisoire?** eskə vōō
	pōōryā sô·änyā lä däN də fäsôN
	prôvēzô·är?

9

| Please don't pull the tooth. | **Je ne veux pas que vous m'arrachiez la dent.** zhə nə vä pä kə vōō märäshyä lä däN. |
| Would you give me/ I'd rather not have an injection, please. | **Faites-moi une injection/Ne me faites pas d'injection,** s'il vous plaît. fet-mô-ä ēn eNzheksyôN/nə mə fet pä deNzheksyôN, sēl vōō ple. |

What the Dentist says

Vous avez besoin ... vōōzävā bəzô-eN ...	You need a ...
d'un bridge. deN brēdzh.	bridge.
d'un plombage. deN plôNbäzh.	filling.
d'une couronne. dẽn kōōrôn.	crown.
Je dois extraire la dent. zhə dô-ä ekstrer lä däN.	I'll have to pull the tooth.
Rincez bien. reNsā byeN.	Rinse out your mouth.
Ne rien manger pendant deux heures, s'il vous plaît. nə rē-eN mäNzhā päNdäN dāzär, sēl vōō ple.	Don't eat anything for two hours.

At the Dentist's

amalgam	**l'amalgame** *m* lämälgäm
bridge	**le bridge** lə brēdzh
cavity	**la carie** lä kärē

crown	**la couronne** lä kōōrôn
gold –	**la couronne en or** lä kōōrôn äNôr
porcelain –	**la couronne en porcelaine** lä kōōrôn äN pôrsəlen
dentist	**le dentiste** lə däNtēst
dentures	**le dentier** lə däNtyä
filling	**le plombage** lə plôNbäzh
temporary –	**le traitement provisoire** lə tretmäN prôvēzô·är
gums	**la gencive** lä zhäNsēv
imprint	**l'empreinte** f läNpreNt
infection	**l'inflammation** f leNflämäsyôN
injection	**l'injection** f leNzheksyôN
jaw	**la mâchoire** lä mäshô·är
local anesthetic	**l'anesthésie** f **locale** länestāzē lôkäl
nerve	**le nerf** lə ner
to pull (a tooth)	**arracher** äräshā
pyorrhea	**la parodontose** lä pärädôntōz
root	**la racine** lä räsēn
-canal work	**le traitement de la racine** lə tretmäN də lä räsēn
tooth	**la dent** lä däN
wisdom –	**la dent de sagesse** lä däN də säzhes

9

POLICE; LOST AND FOUND

Where is the nearest police station?

Où est le poste de police le plus proche? ōō e lə pôst də pôlēs lə plē̄ prôsh?

Does anyone here speak English?

Est-ce qu'il y a ici quelqu'un qui parle anglais? eskēlyä ēsē kelkeN kē pärl äNgle?

I'd like to report a theft.

Je voudrais déposer une plainte pour vol. zhə vōōdre dāpōzā ēn pleNt pōōr vôl.

I'd like to report an accident.

Je voudrais faire une déclaration d'accident. zhə vōōdre fer ēn dāklāräsyôN däksēdäN.

 Breakdown and Accidents (p. 76)

My *daughter/son* has disappeared.

Ma fille/Mon fils a disparu. mä fē'ē/môN fēs ä dēspärē.

My ... has been stolen.

On m'a volé ... ôN mä vôlā ...

I've lost ...

J'ai perdu ... zhā perdē ...

My car has been broken into.

On a ouvert ma voiture par effraction. ôNä ōōver mä vô·tēr pär efräksyôN.

My *house/room* has been broken into.

On a cambriolé ma maison/chambre. ôNä käNbrē·ôlā mä mezôN/shäNb'rə.

I need a copy of the official report for insurance purposes.

J'ai besoin d'une attestation pour mon assurance. zhā bezô·eN dēn ätestäsyôN pōōr môNäsē̄räNs.

224

I'd like to speak to *my lawyer/the consulate*.	**Je voudrais parler *à mon avocat/avec mon consulat.*** zhə vōōdre pärlä ä mônävôkä/ävek môN kôNsēlä.
I'm innocent.	**Je suis ♂ innocent/♀ innocente.** zhə svē ♂ ēnôsäN/♀ ēnôsäNt.

What the Police say

Remplissez ce formulaire. räNplēsä sə fôrmēler.	Please fill out this form.
Votre passeport, s'il vous plaît. vôt'rə päspôr, sēl vōō ple.	Your passport, please.
Quelle est votre adresse aux États-Unis? kel e vôträdres ōzātäzēnē?	What is your address in America?
Où habitez-vous ici? ōō äbētä-vōō ēsē?	Where are you staying here?
***Quand/Où* est-ce que c'est arrivé?** käN/ōō eskə setärēvä?	*When/Where* did this happen?
Contactez votre consulat, s'il vous plaît. kôNtäktä vôt'rə kôNsēlä, sēl vōō ple.	Please get in touch with your consulate.

9

225

accident	**l'accident** *m* läksēdäN
to arrest	**arrêter** ärätā
to break into	**cambrioler** käNbrē·ôlā
car	**la voiture** lä vô·ätēr
– radio	**l'autoradio** *m* lôtôrädyō
– registration	**les papiers** *m/pl* **de voiture** lā päpyā də vô·ätēr
consulate	**le consulat** lə kôNsēlä
handbag	**le sac à main** lə säk ä meN
to harass	**importuner** eNpôrtēnā
ID	**la carte d'identité** lä kärt dēdäNtētā
lawyer	**l'avocat** *m* lävôkä
lost	**perdu** perdē
lost and found	**le bureau des objets trouvés** lə bērō dāzôbzhe trōōvā
mugging	**l'agression** *f* lägresyôN
passport	**le passeport** lə päspôr
police	**la police** lä pôlēs
– officer	**le policier** lə pôlēsyā
– station	**le poste de police** lə pôst də pôlēs
to press charges	**porter plainte** pôrtā pleNt
rape	**le viol** lə vyôl
stolen	**volé** vôlā
theft	**le vol** lə vôl
thief	**le voleur** lə vôlēr
wallet	**le porte-monnaie** lə pôrt-mône
witness	**le témoin** lə tāmô·eN

Time and Weather

TIME

Time of Day

What time is it?	**Quelle heure est-il?** kelǟr etēl?
It's one o'clock.	**Il est une heure.** ēletēnǟr.
It's two o'clock.	**Il est deux heures.** ēl e dǟzǟr.
It's three thirty-five.	**Il est quinze heures trente-cinq.** ēl e keNzǟr träNt-seNk.
It's a quarter past five.	**Il est cinq heures et quart.** ēl e keNzǟr ā kär.
It's six-thirty.	**Il est six heures et demie.** ēl e sēsǟr ā dəmē.
It's a quarter to nine.	**Il est neuf heures moins le quart.** ēl e nēfǟr mô·eN lə kär.
It's five after four.	**Il est quatre heures cinq.** ēl e kätrǟr seNk.
It's ten to eight.	**Il est huit heures moins dix.** ēl e ē·ētǟr mô·eN dēs.
(At) What time?	**A quelle heure?** ä kelǟr?
At ten o'clock.	**A dix heures.** ä dēsǟr.
Around eleven.	**Vers onze heures.** ver ôNzǟr.
Nine o'clock sharp.	**A neuf heures trente précises.** ä nǟfǟr träNt prāsēz.

From eight till nine (o'clock).	**De huit heures à neuf heures.** də ē·ētār ä näfār.
Between ten and twelve.	**Entre dix et douze.** äNt'rə dēs ā dōōz.
Not before seven p.m.	**Pas avant dix-neuf heures.** päsäväN dēs-näfār.
Just after nine o'clock.	**Un peu après neuf heures.** eN pā äpre näfār.
In half an hour.	**Dans une demi-heure.** däNzēn dəmē-ār.
In two hours.	**Dans deux heures.** däN däzār.
It's (too) late.	**Il est (trop) tard.** ēl e (trō) tär.
It's still too early.	**Il est encore trop tôt.** ēl etäNkôr trō tō.

Basic Vocabulary

afternoon	**l'après-midi** *m* läpre-mēdē
in the –	**l'après-midi** *m* läpre-mēdē
this –	**cet après-midi** setäpre-mēdē
ago	**il y a** ēlyä
before	**avant** äväN
day	**le jour** lə zhōōr
every –	**tous les jours** tōō lā zhōōr
earlier	**plus tôt** plē tō
early	**tôt** tō
evening	**le soir** lə sô·är

in the –	**le soir** lə sô·är
this –	**ce soir** sə sô·är
every week	**chaque semaine** shäk səmēn
hour	**l'heure** *f* lär
every –	**toutes les heures** tōōt lāzär
half an –	**la demi-heure** lä dəmē-är
quarter of an –	**le quart d'heure** lə kär där
late	**tard** tär
later	**plus tard** plē tär
minute	**la minute** lä mēnēt
month	**le mois** lə mô·ä
morning	**le matin** lə mäteN
in the –	**le matin** lə mätəN
this –	**ce matin** sə mäteN
night	**la nuit** lä nē̈·ē
at –	**la nuit** lä nē̈·ē
last –	**hier soir** yer sô·är
noon	**midi** mēdē
at –	**à midi** ä mēdē
at – today	**ce midi** sə mēdē
now	**maintenant** meNtnäN
recently	**récemment** rāsämäN
since	**depuis** dəpē̈·ē
sometimes	**quelquefois** kelkəfô·ä
soon	**bientôt** byeNtō
time	**le temps** lə täN
in/on –	**à temps** ä täN
today	**aujourd'hui** ōzhōōrdvē
tomorrow	**demain** dəmeN

230

the day after –	**après-demain** äpre-dəmeN
tonight	**cette nuit, ce soir** set nē·ē, sə sô·är
until	**jusqu'à** zhēskä
week	**la semaine** lä səmen
in two weeks	**dans quinze jours** däN keNz zhōōr
weekend	**le week-end** lə ōō·ēk-end
on the –	**le week-end** lə ōō·ēk-end
year	**l'année** *f* länā
last –	**l'année** *f* **dernière** länā dernyer
next –	**l'année** *f* **prochaine** länā prôshen
yesterday	**hier** yer
the day before –	**avant-hier** äväNtyer

Seasons

spring	**le printemps** lə preNtäN
summer	**l'été** *m* lātā
fall	**l'automne** *m* lôtôn
winter	**l'hiver** *m* lēver

Legal Holidays

All Saints' Day	**la Toussaint** lä tōōseN
Christmas	**Noël** nô·el
Christmas Eve	**la veille de Noël** lä ve'ē də nô·el
Easter	**Pâques** päk
Mardi gras	**le carnaval** lə kärnäväl
New Year	**le jour de l'an** lə zhōōr də läN
New Year's Eve	**la Saint-Sylvestre** lä seN-sēlvest'rə

10

INFO Bastille Day on July 14 is a national holiday in France. It is celebrated with parades and dances in the evening. Other holidays include May 8 (the end of World War II) and November 11 (Armistice Day, end of World War I).

THE DATE

What's today's date?	**On est le combien aujourd'hui?** ôNe lə kôNbyeN ōzhōōrdvē?
Today is July 2.	**Aujourd'hui, on est le deux juillet.** ōzhōōrdvē, ôNe lə dœ̄ zhē-ēye.
I was born on August 24, 1971.	**Je suis né le vingt-quatre août 1971.** zhə svē nā lə veN-kätrōōt mēl näf säN sô-äsäNtä-eN.
On the 4th of *this/next* month.	**Le quatre *de ce mois/du mois pro-chain*.** lə kät'rə də sə mô-ä/dᵫ mô-ä prōsheN.
Until March 10.	**Jusqu'au dix mars.** zhēskō dē märs.
We're leaving on August 20.	**Nous partons le vingt août.** nōō pärtôN lə veNtōōt.
We arrived on July 25.	**Nous sommes arrivés le vingt-cinq juillet.** nōō sôm ärēvā lə veN-seNk zhē-ēye.

232

Days of the Week

Monday	**lundi** leNdē
Tuesday	**mardi** märdē
Wednesday	**mercredi** merkrədē
Thursday	**jeudi** zhə̄dē
Friday	**vendredi** väNdrədē
Saturday	**samedi** sämdē
Sunday	**dimanche** dēmäNsh

Months

January	**janvier** zhäNvyā
February	**février** fāvrē-ā
March	**mars** märs
April	**avril** ävrēl
May	**mai** me
June	**juin** zhə̄-eN
July	**juillet** zhē-ēye
August	**août** ōōt
September	**septembre** septäNb'rə
October	**octobre** ôktôb'rə
November	**novembre** nôväNb'rə
December	**décembre** dāsäNb'rə

10

THE WEATHER

What's the weather going to be like today?	**Quel temps va-t-il faire aujourd'hui?** kel täN vätēl fer ōzhōōrdvē?

Have you heard the weather forecast?	**Vous avez déjà écouté la météo?** vōōzävä dāzhä ākōōtā lä mätä-ō?

It's going to *be/get* ... **Il *fait/va faire* ...** ēl fe/vä fer ...

warm.	**chaud.** shō.
hot.	**très chaud.** tre shō.
cold.	**froid.** frô·ä.
cool.	**frais.** fre.
humid.	**lourd.** lōōr.

It's rather windy.	**Il y a pas mal de vent.** ēlyä pä mäl də väN.

It's very windy.	**Il y a de la tempête.** ēlyä də lä täNpet.

What's the temperature?	**Quelle est la température?** kel e lä täNpärätēr?

It's ... degrees *above/below* zero.	**Il fait ... degrés *au-dessus/au-dessous* de zéro.** ēl fe ... dəgrā ōdəsē/ōdəsōō də zärō.

It looks like *rain/a storm*.	**On dirait qu'il va *pleuvoir/faire de l'orage*.** ôN dēre kēl vä plə̱vô·är/fer də lôräzh.

air	**l'air** *m* lĕr
blizzard	**la tempête de neige** lä täNpät də nezh
clear	**clair** klĕr
climate	**le climat** lə klēmä
cloud	**le nuage** lə nē·äzh
cold	**froid** frô·ä
I'm –	**j'ai froid** zhā frô·ä
cool	**frais,** *f:* **fraîche** fre, *f:* fresh
degree	**le degré** lə dəgrā
dry	**sec,** *f:* **sèche** sek, *f:* sesh
fair *(weather)*	**beau** bō
fog	**le brouillard** lə brōōyär
it's freezing	**il gèle** ēl zhel
frost	**le gel** lə zhel
it's hailing	**il grêle** ēl grel
hazy	**brumeux** brēmə̄
heat	**la grosse chaleur** lä grōs shälœr
high-pressure area	**l'anticyclone** *m* läNtēsēklôn
hot	**chaud** shō
I'm –	**j'ai chaud** zhā shō
humid	**humide** ēmēd
ice *(on the roads)*	**le verglas** lə verglä
lightning	**les éclairs** *m/pl* lāzākler
low-pressure area	**la dépression** lä dāpresyôN
moon	**la lune** lä lēn
overcast	**nuageux** nē·äzhə̄
precipitation	**les précipitations** *f/pl* lā prāsēpētäsyôN
rain	**la pluie** lä plē·ē

10

235

it's raining	**il pleut** ēl plœ
shower *(of rain)*	**l'averse** *f* lävers
snow	**la neige** lä nezh
it's snowing	**il neige** ēl nezh
star	**l'étoile** *f* lātô-äl
storm	**la tempête** lä täNpet
it's stormy	**il y a de la tempête** ēlyä də lä täNpet
sultry *(weather)*	**lourd** lōōr
sun	**le soleil** lə sôle'ē
sunny	**ensoleillé** äNsôläyā
sunrise	**le lever du soleil** lə ləvā dē sôle'ē
sunset	**le coucher du soleil** lə kōōshā dē sôle'ē
temperature	**la température** lä täNpārätēr
thaw	**le dégel** lə dāzhel
it's thawing	**c'est le dégel** se lə dāzhel
it's thundering	**il tonne** ēl tôn
thunderstorm	**l'orage** *m* lôräzh
variable	**capricieux** käprēsyœ
warm	**chaud** shō
weather	**le temps** lə täN
– forecast	**la météo** lä mātā-ō
wet	**mouillé** mōōyā
wind	**le vent** lə väN
– strength	**la force du vent** lä fôrs dē väN
it's windy	**il y a du vent** ēlyä dē väN

Grammar

ARTICLES

Definite and Indefinite Articles

As with most other foreign languages, French divides nouns into genders: nouns and their preceding articles are either *masculine* or *feminine*.

	Singular		Plural	
	♂	♀	♂	♀
Definite Article	**le jour** the day	**la nuit** the night	**les jours** the days	**les nuits** the nights
Indefinite Article	**un jour** a day	**une nuit** a night	**des jours** days	**des nuits** nights

When followed by a word starting with a vowel or the silent **h**, the articles **le** and **la** abbreviate into **l'**: **l'avion** – the airplane, **l'adresse** – the address, **l'hotel** – the hotel.

When used together with the prepositions **à** and **de**, the articles **le** and **les** contract as follows:

à + le → au   à + les → aux
de + le → du   de + les → des

Exception: **l'** does not change or form a contraction:
Je vais à l'hôtel.   I'm going to the hotel.
Je viens de l'hôtel.   I'm coming from the hotel.

Partitive Articles and Amounts

If you wish to indicate an indefinite amount of something, you must use the so-called partitive articles. These are formed by using the preposition **de** together with the definite article.

| Singular | | Plural | |
♂	♀	♂	♀
du pain	**de la bière**	**des jours**	**des pommes**
(some) bread	(some) beer	days	apples

On the other hand, if you wish to denote a definite amount, you must couple the nouns with **de**. **Beaucoup** (many/a lot of) and **peu** (few) also count as a "definite amount."

| Singular | | Plural | |
♂	♀	♂	♀
une bouteille de lait	**un litre d'eau**	**un kilo d'abricots**	**un kilo de pommes**
a bottle of milk	a liter of water	a kilo of apricots	a kilo of apples

NOUNS

The Cases

The nominative and dative cases are identical in form. The genitive is formed with the help of the preposition **de**, the dative case with the propositon **à**.

Nominative	**Où est la gare?** Where is the station?
Genitive	**Où est la maison de ton oncle?** Where is your uncle's house?
Dative	**Je montre mon billet au contrôleur.** I show the inspector my ticket.
Accusative	**Je cherche la rue Mouffetard.** I'm looking for the Rue Mouffetard.

Plurals

1. As in English, the plural is almost always formed by the addition of an **-s**; however, this **-s** remains silent.
2. Words ending in **-al** usually form the plural using **-aux**.
   le journal – the newspaper → **les journaux**
3. One important irregular plural is **l'oeil** – the eye → **les yeux**. Note the pronounciation of the plural of **l'œuf** [lǣf] – the egg → **les œufs** [lāzā].

ADJECTIVES AND ADVERBS

Adjectives

Adjectives conform to the nouns they modify in both gender and number.

An adjective is usually put into the feminine by adding an **-e** to the end of the masculine form. Some adjectives change slightly to accommodate this: the last consonant may be doubled, for example **-el → -elle** (**officiel → officielle**) or an accent mark will be added to the last vowel, for example **-ier → -ière** (**premier → première**). These changes are also noteworthy: **-eux** and **-eur →** **-euse**, **-if → -ive**, **-eau → -elle**. If the masculine form already ends in an **-e**, then the adjective remains unchanged in the feminine. As with the nouns, the plural is generally made by adding an **-s** to the singular form.

Singular		Plural	
♂	♀	♂	♀
Le parc est grand.	**La ville est grande.**	**Les parcs sont grands.**	**Les villes sont grandes.**
The park is large.	The town is big.	The parks are large.	The towns are big.

Adjectives are usually placed after the noun:
un film intéressant   an interesting film
la veste verte   the green jacket

Short adjectives are generally placed before the noun. These include **bon** (good), **beau** (handsome/beautiful), **joli** (pretty), **jeune** (young), **vieux** (old), **grand** (large), and **petit** (small):

un bon repas   a good meal

Adverbs

Adverbs are formed by adding **-ment** to the end of the female adjective form:

froid – cold → **froide** → **froidement** – coldly.

There are also adverbs that do not derive from the adjective form; the most important ones are:

bien – well, **mal** – badly, **vite** – fast, **beaucoup** – much.

Comparatives

Adjectives and adverbs are intensified for the comparative by putting the word **plus** in front of them; the superlative is formed by using the comparative with a definite article:

grand	→	**plus grand (que)**	→	**le plus grand**
large		larger (than)		the largest
beau	→	**plus beau (que)**	→	**le plus beau**
handsome		handsomer (than)		the handsomest

Nicolas est plus beau que Lucas.
Nicolas is handsomer than Lucas.
Paris est la plus belle ville du monde.
Paris is the most beautiful city in the world.

PRONOUNS

Personal Pronouns

1. normal

	Nominative		Indirect Object		Direct Object	
Singular	**je**	I	**me**	(to) me	**me**	me
	tu	you	**te**	(to) you	**te**	you
	il	he	**lui**	(to) him	**le**	him/it
	elle	she		(to) her	**la**	her
Plural	**nous**	we	**nous**	(to) us	**nous**	us
	vous	you	**vous**	(to) you	**vous**	you
	ils	they ♂	**leur**	(to) them	**les**	them
	elles	they ♀				

On is often used instead of **nous** in casual speech: **On y va?** – Shall we go?

2. emphasized

Singular		Plural	
moi	I	**nous**	we
toi	you	**vous**	you
lui	he	**eux**	they ♂
elle	she	**elles**	they ♀

The emphasized forms are used as follows:

1. When they stand by themselves: **mon frère et moi** – my brother and I.
2. After prepositions: **sans toi** – without you.
3. To emphasize someone or something: **Lui, il est déjà parti.** – *He* is already gone.

Reflexive Pronouns

	Direct and Indirect Object	
Singular	**me**	myself
	te	yourself
	se	oneself
Plural	**nous**	ourselves
	vous	yourselves
	se	oneselves

In the French language, many actions refer back to the subject of the action in the form of reflexive verbs: **Je me lave les mains.** – I am washing my hands. **Nous nous levons à 8 heures.** – We get up at 8 o'clock.

Y and en

Y and **en** can replace the names of locations used with **à** and **de**, respectively:

Il va à Paris?	Is he going to Paris?
Oui, il y va.	Yes, he's going there.
Tu es à Tours?	Are you in Tours?
Oui, j'y suis.	Yes, I'm there.
Je viens de Paris.	I come from Paris.
J'en viens.	I come from there.

Y and **en** can also replace phrases beginning with **à** and **de**:

Tu pense à faire la vaisselle?	Will you remember to do the dishes?
J'y pense.	I'll remember to do it.
Il a mangé de la tarte?	Did he eat some of the tart?
Oui, il en a mangé.	Yes, he ate some of it.

Pronoun Placement

Pronouns are placed before the verb in this order:

me			
te	le		
se	la	lui	
nous	les	leur	y, en
vous			

245

For example:
Je vous le rends. I give it back to you.
Je lui en parle. I speak to him about it.

Possessive Pronouns

'Possession'	Singular		Plural
'Possessor'	♂	♀	♂ and ♀
Singular	**mon** **ton** fils **son**	**ma** **ta** fille **sa**	**mes** **tes** **ses** **enfants**
Plural	**notre** **votre** fils, fille **leur**		**nos** **vos** **leurs**

The gender of the possessive pronoun always agrees with what is referred to as belonging to the subject of the sentence and not with the subject itself: **son fils** – his/her son, **sa fille** – his/her daughter.

In these examples it is not clear whether the parent in question is the mother or the father.

Note: Words that begin with a vowel or with the silent **h** always take the masculine personal pronouns **mon**, **ton** and **son**: **mon amie** – my (female) friend, **son histoire** – his/her story.

Demonstrative Pronouns

Singular		Plural	
♂	♀	♂	♀
ce pain	**cette pomme**	**ces pains**	**ces pommes**
this bread	this apple	these breads	these apples

Note: masculine words that begin with a vowel or the silent **h** use
the demonstrative pronoun **cet**: **cet ami** – this friend, **cet hôtel** –
this hotel.

The word for "that" and "it" in French is **cela**; it is often con-
tracted to **ça**:

Cela/Ça me plaît.   I like it/that.

When placed before **être** (to be), **ce** means "that" or "it" (singular) or "they" or "those" (plural):

c'est ...   that/it is ...
ce sont ...   they/those are ...

Relative Pronouns

qui (nominative): **Je prends le train qui part à 8 heures.** – I'm
taking the train that leaves at 8 o'clock.
que (accusative): **C'est l'homme que j'ai vu.** – That's the man
that I saw.

VERBS

The most important tenses are:

The Present Tense: It expresses actions and situations taking place in the present: **Nicolas regarde son père.** – Nicolas is looking at his father.

The Future Tense: It expresses actions and situations in the future: **Demain, nous partirons en vacances.** – Tomorrow we are going on vacation.

You can put a verb in the future by using the infinitive (minus the final **-e**) and the proper ending: **donner + ai → donnerai; mettr(e) + ai → mettrai.** You can also express the future by using the present tense of **aller** (to go) with the infinitive: **Demain, nous allons partir en vacances.** – Tomorrow we are going to go on vacation.

The Past Tense: It expresses a situation or a repeated action in the past. It is formed by taking the root of the first person plural in the present tense and the proper ending: **finiss(ons) + ais → finissais.**

The Perfect Tense: It expresses a single, short-lived and/or sudden action in the past: **Nicolas lisait; tout à coup, le téléphone a sonné.** – Nicolas was reading; suddenly the phone rang. The perfect is usually formed by adding the past participle to the present of **avoir**: **j'ai + montré → j'ai montré.**
Reflexive verbs and action verbs, however, form the perfect with **être** instead of **avoir**: **Je suis allé au cinéma.** – I went to the movie theater.

You will frequently encounter the use of the Conditional: It expresses possibility and is often used in polite questions and - responses: **Vous pourriez me montrer ce livre?** – Could you show me this book? You will also need the conditional to make "ifthen" sentences: **Si j'avais assez d'argent, je t'en donnerais.** – If I had enough money I would give you some. As with the future tense, you can put a verb in the conditional by using the infinitive (minus the final **-e**) and adding the appropriate ending: **donner + ais → donnerais.**

Regular Verbs

In French verbs are classified by their infinitive endings:

1. Verbs ending in **-er**
2. Verbs ending in **-ir**
3. Verbs ending in **-re**

Most verbs belong to the first group.

	-er	**-ir**	**-re**
Infinitive	**donner** give	**finir** finish	**mettre** put
Present Tense	**je donne**	**je finis**	**je mets**
	tu donnes	**tu finis**	**tu mets**
	il donne	**il finit**	**il met**
	nous donnons	**nous finissons**	**nous mettons**
	vous donnez	**vous finissez**	**vous mettez**
	ils donnent	**ils finissent**	**ils mettent**

	-er	-ir	-re
Future Tense	je donnerai	je finirai	je mettrai
	tu donneras	tu finiras	tu mettras
	il donnera	il finira	il mettra
	nous donnerons	nous finirons	nous mettrons
	vous donnerez	vous finirez	vous mettrez
	ils donneront	ils finiront	ils mettront
Past Tense	je donnais	je finissais	je mettais
	tu donnais	tu finissais	tu mettais
	il donnait	il finissait	il mettait
	nous donnions	nous finissions	nous mettions
	vous donniez	vous finissiez	vous mettiez
	ils donnaient	ils finissaient	ils mettaient
Perfect Tense	j'ai donné	j'ai fini	j'ai mis*
	tu as donné	tu as fini	tu as mis
	il a donné	il a fini	il a mis
	nous avons donné	nous avons fini	nous avons mis
	vous avez donné	vous avez fini	vous avez mis
	ils ont donné	ils ont fini	ils ont mis
Conditional	je donnerais	je finirais	je mettrais
	tu donnerais	tu finirais	tu mettrais
	il donnerait	il finirait	il mettrait
	nous donnerions	nous finirions	nous mettrions
	vous donneriez	vous finiriez	vous mettriez
	ils donneraient	ils finiraient	ils mettraient

*mettre: irregular past participle: mis.

avoir and *être*

	avoir have	**être** be
Present Tense	j'ai tu as il a nous avons vous avez ils ont	je suis tu es il est nous sommes vous êtes ils sont
Future Tense	j'aurai tu auras il aura nous aurons vous aurez ils auront	je serai tu seras il sera nous serons vous serez ils seront
Past Tense	j'avais tu avais il avait nous avions vous aviez ils avaient	j'étais tu étais il était nous étions vous étiez ils étaient
Perfect Tense	j'ai eu tu as eu il a eu nous avons eu vous avez eu ils ont eu	j'ai été tu as été il a été vous avez été vous avez été ils ont été

	avoir have	être be
Conditional	j'aurais	je serais
	tu aurais	tu serais
	il aurait	il serait
	nous aurions	nous serions
	vous auriez	vous seriez
	ils auraient	ils seraient

Irregular Verbs

Here are the most frequently used irregular verbs conjugated in the present tense together with their further irregular forms:

aller go

Present Tense: **je vais, tu vas, il va, nous allons, vous allez, ils vont**

Future Tense: **j'irai, tu iras** etc.

Perfect Tense: **je suis allé, tu es allé** etc.

Conditional: **j'irais, tu irais** etc.

boire drink

Present Tense: **je bois, tu bois, il boit, nous buvons, vous buvez, ils boivent**

Perfect Tense: **j'ai bu, tu as bu** etc.

Conditional: **je boirais, tu boirais** etc.

devoir have to

Present Tense: **je dois, tu dois, il doit, nous devons, vous devez, ils doivent**

Future Tense: **je devrai, tu devras** etc.

| Perfect Tense: | **j'ai dû, tu as dû** etc. |
| Conditional: | **je devrais, tu devrais** etc. |

faire do

Present Tense:	**je fais, tu fais, il fait, nous faisons, vous faites, ils font**
Future Tense:	**je ferai, tu feras** etc.
Perfect Tense:	**j'ai fait, tu as fait** etc.
Conditional:	**je ferais, tu ferais** etc.

pouvoir can

Present Tense:	**je peux, tu peux, il peut, nous pouvons, vous pouvez, ils peuvent**
Future Tense:	**je pourrai, tu pourras** etc.
Perfect Tense:	**j'ai pu, tu as pu** etc.
Conditional:	**je pourrais, tu pourrais** etc.

prendre take

Present Tense:	**je prends, tu prends, il prend, nous prenons, vous prenez, ils prennent**
Perfect Tense:	**j'ai pris, tu as pris** etc.
Conditional:	**je prendrais, tu prendrais** etc.

savoir know

Present Tense:	**je sais, tu sais, il sait, nous savons, vous savez, ils savent**
Future Tense:	**je saurai, tu sauras** etc.
Perfect Tense:	**j'ai su, tu as su** etc.
Conditional:	**je saurais, tu saurais** etc.

venir come

Present Tense: **je viens, tu viens, il vient, nous venons, vous venez, ils viennent**

Future Tense: **je viendrai, tu viendras** etc.

Perfect Tense: **je suis venu, tu es venu** etc.

Conditional: **je viendrais, tu viendrais** etc.

vouloir want to

Present Tense: **je veux, tu veux, il veut, nous voulons, vous voulez, ils veulent**

Future Tense: **je voudrai, tu voudras** etc.

Conditional: **je voudrais, tu voudrais** etc.

NEGATIVE SENTENCES

The negative is expressed by using the word **ne** together with another word such as **pas**, **plus**, etc. These words surround the verb. In casual speech, however, the **ne** is often left out, so that the subsequent words **pas**, **plus**, etc. express the negation.

1. not: **ne ... pas**

   Ce n'est pas ma valise.   That is not my suitcase.

2. nothing/not anything: **ne ... rien**

   Il n'a rien à manger.   He has nothing to eat./He doesn't have anything to eat.

3. no more/not any more: **ne ... plus**

   Il n'y a plus d'essence.   There's no more gas./There isn't any more gas.

4. nobody/not anybody: **ne ... personne**
   Je n'y ai vu personne.   I saw nobody there./I didn't see
                                    anybody there.

5. never: **ne ... jamais**
   Il ne fait jamais la   He never washes the dishes.
   vaisselle.

INTERROGATIVE SENTENCES

How to ask questions:

There are generally three ways to form interrogative sentences:

1. Using the word **est-ce que**:
   Est-ce que tu es contente? Are you happy?

2. Transposing the subject and verb:
   Es-tu contente?   Are you happy?

3. Using rising inflection at the end of the sentence:
   Tu es contente?   Are you happy?

Interrogative Pronouns

The most important interrogative pronouns are:

| when | **quand** | **Quand est-ce qu'il arrive?** When does he arrive? |
| why | **pourquoi** | **Pourquoi est-ce qu'elle ne vient pas?** Why doesn't she come? |

what	qu'est-ce qui	**Qu'est-ce qui se passe?** What has happened?
	qu'est-ce que	**Qu'est-ce que nous faisons demain?** What are we going to do tomorrow?
which	quel, *f*: quelle	**Quelle salade prendrez-vous?** Which salad are you taking?
who(m)	a qui	**À qui vous avez donné vos clés?** Who(m) did you give your keys?
who(m)	qui	**Qui voulez-vous voir?** Who(m) would you like to see?
who	qui	**Qui vient avec nous?** Who is coming with us?
how	comment	**Comment vas-tu?** How are you?
how long	combien de temps	**Combien de temps dure le voyage?** How long does the journey take?
how much	combien	**Combien coûte le billet?** How much is the ticket?
where	où	**Où sont les toilettes?** Where are the rest rooms?
what ... of	à quoi	**À quoi penses-tu?** What are you thinking of?
what ... about	de quoi	**De quoi parlez-vous?** What are you talking about?
who(m) ... about	de qui	**De qui parlez-vous?** Who(m) are you talking about?

NUMBERS

Cardinal Numbers

0	zéro	zārō
1	un	eN
2	deux	dᾳ
3	trois	trô·ä
4	quatre	kät'rə
5	cinq	seNk
6	six	sēs
7	sept	set
8	huit	ē·ēt
9	neuf	nᾳf
10	dix	dēs
11	onze	ôNz
12	douze	dōōz
13	treize	trez
14	quatorze	kätôrz
15	quinze	keNz
16	seize	sez
17	dix-sept	dēset
18	dix-huit	dēzē·ēt
19	dix-neuf	dēznᾳf
20	vingt	veN
21	vingt et un	veNtā·eN
22	vingt-deux	veNt-dᾳ
23	vingt-trois	veNt-trô·ä
24	vingt-quatre	veNt-kät'rə
25	vingt-cinq	veNt-seNk

26	vingt-six veNt-sēs
27	vingt-sept veNt-set
28	vingt-huit veNtē̠-ēt
29	vingt-neuf veNt-nạf
30	trente träNt
40	quarante kåräNt
50	cinquante seNkäNt
60	soixante sô·äsäNt
70	soixante-dix sô·äsäNtdēs
80	quatre-vingts kätrəveN
90	quatre-vingt-dix kätrəveNdēs
100	cent säN
101	cent un säN eN
579	cinq cent soixante-dix-neuf seNk säN sô·äsänt-dēs-nạf
1000	mille mēl
2000	deux mille dạ̈ mēl
10 000	dix mille dēs mēl

Ordinal Numbers

1st	premier prəmyā
2nd	deuxième dạ̈zyem
3rd	troisième trô·äzyem
4th	quatrième kätrēyem
5th	cinquième seNkyem
6th	sixième sēsyem
7th	septième setyem
8th	huitième ē̠-ētyem
9th	neuvième nạ̈fyem

Here.	**Qui.** kōō·ē'.
There.	**Là.** lä.
On/To the right.	**A destra.** ä des'trä.
On/To the left.	**A sinistra.** ä sēnēs'trä.
Straight ahead.	**Sempre diritto.** sem'pre dērē'tō.
Do you have …?	**Ha …?** ä …?
I would like …	**Vorrei …** vōre'ē …
How much does this cost?	**Quanto costa?** kōō·än'tō kō'stä?
Could you please write that down for me?	**Me lo può scrivere, per favore?** me lō pōō·ō' skrē'vere, per fävō're?
Where is …?	**Dov'è …?** dōve' …?
Where *is/are* there …?	***Dov'è/Dove sono …?*** dōve'/dō've sō'nō …?
Today.	**Oggi.** ō'jē.
Tomorrow.	**Domani.** dōmä'nē.
I don't want to.	**Non voglio.** nōn vō'lyō.
I can't.	**Non posso.** nōn pō'sō.
Just a minute, please.	**Un momento, per favore!** ōōn mōmen'tō, per fävō're!
Leave me alone!	**Mi lasci in pace!** mē lä'shē ēn pä'tshe!

Name
Nome
Home address
Indirizzo di residenza

Date of birth
Data di nascita
Vacation address
Indirizzo di vacanza

ID/passport no.
Numero *della carta d'identità/del passaporto*

In case of emergency, please contact:
In caso di emergenza avvisare:

Important information (allergies, medicines, blood type, etc.)
**Informazioni importanti (allergie, farmaci,
gruppo sanguigno ecc.)**

In case of lost traveler's checks, please contact:

In case of lost credit cards, please contact: